SUNDANCE AND CHEROKEE MOON:

ABOUT ROBERT REDFORD, MOVIES

MEDJUGORJE, MIRACLES AND MANIA

MY SPIRITUAL TRIUMPH

WITH BI-POLAR ILLNESS

MARY KAY GREEN, J.D.

Sundance and Cherokee Moon

Book Cover: Original graphic cover artist, Linda Darlene Behl Brennaman, Volunteer Intern at UMKC Bookmark Press (editorial assistant, cover artist, illustrator, graphic designer, promotional marketing designer) 2011 through 2013, Kansas City, MO. lindricks@prodigy.net.

Editor: Joan Sheehan, M.A. Psychology, Omaha, NE, retired principal of twenty years at Our Lady of Lourdes Parish, Denver, CO. choan@cox.net. Omaha, NE.

Mary Kay Green, J.D. author
c/o Mary Kay Green, Jr.
402 NE Corder Street
Lees Summit, MO 64063

mkgkansascity17@gmail.com

OTHER WORKS BY THE AUTHOR

Also for publication in 2015

At Will/No Deal: The Civil Rights Law Exceptions to At Will Employment: The Real Employee Handbook, Mary Kay Green, J.D. The Author's practice included the enforcement of all federal employment discrimination laws in over twenty years as a Plaintiffs' Employment Discrimination Attorney. Every employee should have two copies, one for you and one to take to your lawyer.

They Let Mothers in Law School? This is an easily readable screenplay based on the author's three years in law school from 1974 to 1977 at Creighton University Law School in Omaha, NE. In 1974 there were 30 women law students in the 180 student freshman class—the first large class of women. Ten of these women were mothers—the first mothers to go to Creighton Law School. The single mother law student author and her two mother law student friends in her study group were part of the ten. The screenplay is both serious and hilarious.

Published in 2007.

Women of Courage: The Rights of Single Mothers and Their Children Inspired by Crystal Chambers a New Rosa Parks. Based on Crystal Chambers' famous race, sex and single pregnancy discrimination lawsuit against the Omaha Girls Club between 1982 through 1988, this book chronicles the lives of Rosa Parks, Crystal Chambers' role model, Crystal Chambers herself, and her single parent lawyer, the author. After a "loud voice" prophecy by an Omaha Catholic priest to the lawyer/author, the case was covered by the national media in *The New Your Times, twice on NPR's All Things Considered, in Newsweek, The New York Daily News, in In These Times, The Lincoln Journal Star* in Lincoln, NE, *The Omaha World Herald,* and Ms. Chambers and her attorney appeared on the Phil Donahue television talk show *Donahue,* all in 1986 and in 2003, Crystal Chambers and her case were featured on *The Tom Joyner Show* ,a nationally syndicated radio talk show, in his half hour segment titled: "*Little Known Black Heroes.*" Over a hundred law review articles have been written about this case and it is taught in the *Employment Law* text book used in America's law schools.

3

AUTHOR'S NOTE

There is a Psychiatric Museum in St. Joseph, MO. The physical exhibits in that museum show the tortures that people with mental illness have been subjected to from the early days in Europe to the years in the United States. The museum is open to the public and the exhibits include a surgery room display and the instruments used to perform lobotomies on persons with mental illness including Rosemary Kennedy, President John F. Kennedy's younger sister. The exhibits in the museum and the outrageous treatment of persons with mental illness should be in a documentary.

Table of Contents

FORWARD

Dear Readers, in the following pages, you will learn of the personal story if you will of a valiant woman, a WOMAN OF COURAGE, Mary Kay Green. I first met Mary Kay when we were freshman at Mercy High in Omaha, Nebraska. We "ran around in the same crowd," a fairly large crowd of "Mercy Girls" and mostly Creighton Prep fellows. It was in the days of the Bunny Hop and "Until the Twelfth of Never," sock hops and picnics at Peony Park and planning our futures, our realities mixed with just a twinge of fantasy so easily embraced by happy high schoolers.

It was in the days of JFK (President John F. Kennedy), with strong Democratic hopes and yearnings for success and fairness for all. Mary Kay's dad, James F. Green, was the working Nebraska co-chairman for John F. Kennedy's Presidential campaign in 1960 and later in 1968 for the U.S. Senator Robert F. Kennedy Presidential campaign and we reveled in Mary Kay's fortune to associate with JFK and his brother Robert F. Kennedy (who would become important later in her life).

We were good kids and smart, ready to take on the world wherever we were led, and for many of us, that meant we were led straight to the Motherhouse of the Sisters of Mercy, but that's for another book. Our training was for hard work and striving for success at whatever we did, taking us into a variety of leadership positions, Social Work, Education and Law. That last is what Mary Kay aspired to and with which she became inured. She dug deeply into Civil Rights cases, from D.C. to the South, then to the Midwest all while raising twin girls as a single mother and dealing with her own demons as a bi-polar woman.

You will find her story fascinating, sometimes unbelievable but true, and always captivating. She tells her story with love and a dedication to peeling off the layers of bi-polar illness, so often misunderstood. Dear Readers, learn of Mary Kay Green,

Joan Sheehan, M.A, Psychologist.

DEDICATION

I dedicate this book to my daughters Elizabeth and Mary Kay and my grandchildren Michael and Miss Phelan, to my late mother and father Betty and Jimmy Green and all my family and friends who have been so important in my life.

I also want to thank my mentors Jack Canfield of the *Chicken Soup* series and *The Success Principles* and Steve Harrison of Bradley Communications who encouraged me to tell my story and taught me how to do it. And to Oprah Winfrey who introduced me to so many spiritual leaders and people who survived and triumphed over life's tragedies and who is such an inspiration to me and millions worldwide.

I want to thank the women and men scientists at Pfizer and at Glaxo Smith Kline who developed Geodon and Lamictal respectively which I started taking in 2004 and which gave me back my life with normal moods with my bi-polar illness, and my psychiatrist A. Mohammed Mirza, M.D., who put me on these meds and has been my psychiatrist since 2004.

I want to thank heroic equal pay champion Lilly Ledbetter (who I got to meet and talk with along with my grandson Michael in the summer 0f 2012 when she came to Kansas City to campaign for the re-election of President Barack Obama). Lilly Ledbetter is the plaintiff in <u>Lilly Ledbetter</u> v <u>Good Year Tire and Rubber Co.</u>, an equal pay case where the U.S. Supreme Court denied her relief by saying that the 180 day filing period under the Equal Pay Act ended with her first discriminatory pay check even though pay records were confidential and an employee could be fired for inquiring about them. She is the same Lilly Ledbetter in the Lilly Ledbetter Fair Pay Act of 2009 reversing the U.S. Supreme Court decision. The act restores the Equal Pay Act and further mandates that each discriminatory paycheck starts the 180 day filing period for a civil rights action. The Lilly Ledbetter Fair Pay Act was the first legislation President Obama signed into law January 29, 2009, right after his swearing in as President January 20, 2009.

I want to thank all plaintiffs in civil rights cases especially my own clients—all of whom showed tremendous courage and fortitude in seeking justice. I want to thank Lilly Ledbetter's lawyers who worked without fees all those ten years and all plaintiffs' civil rights attorneys especially Ed Fogarty and the late Ed Diedrich who assisted me without pay in the trial and appeal of my courageous client Crystal Chambers, now known as married Crystal Chambers Stewart. Without the courage of all these plaintiffs and all these plaintiffs' civil rights lawyers the law would be unenforceable and meaningless.

I want to thank the late Chief Judge of the Eighth Circuit Court of Appeals Donald P. Lay for his dissenting opinion in <u>Crystal Chambers</u> v. <u>Omaha Girls Club.</u> He later wrote to me and encouraged me to write a book about Crystal Chambers' case. I did as he asked and the book's published title is *Women of Courage: The Rights of Single Mothers and Their Children Inspired by Crystal Chambers a New Rosa Parks, by Mary Kay Green, J.D.*

Lastly, I want to thank the late Fr. Thomas Halley, S.J. who took my mother and me to Medjugorje where our lives were changed forever and Monsignor William Whelan, my former spiritual advisor and the Poor Clare Sisters of Omaha who have been friends with my family from the 1930's on and who have been praying for all of us since then. All these holy individuals, all of Omaha, guided my spiritual life and befriended me and my mother.

SUNDANCE AND CHEROKEE MOON:

ABOUT ROBERT REDFORD, MOVIES,

MEDJUGORJE, MIRACLES AND MANIA

My Spiritual Triumph with Bi-Polar Illness

By: Mary Kay Green, J.D., "M.D."

INTRODUCTION:

I am writing this book telling my story and the story of some of the people in my life like an old Irish story teller in the ancient days. I envision we are sitting around a fire, this time indoors in your living room, where I wind my tale with questions from you as the night grows on.

I am finishing this story or memoir in 2015. There are years in our lives that are pivotal. For me 1988 is one of those years. A passionate movie goer, I started the year in January fulfilling a dream by going to the United States Film Festival sponsored by Robert Redford's Sundance Film Institute. (Now the festival is called the Sundance Film Festival.) In the months after that I settled some of my plaintiffs' civil rights cases and with my friend Elizabeth Kountze participated in a six week civil rights trial against the City of Omaha.

With some of that fee, in October, I took my mother Betty Phelan Green to Medjugorje (a village in then Yugoslavia now the Republic of Bosnia Herzegovina) where the Blessed Mother of Jesus has been appearing since June 24, 1981, to six young people called visionaries. The Blessed Mother continues to appear daily even now to three of the visionaries all of whom were young when she first appeared to them. She appears at other time to the other three.

Sundance and Cherokee Moon

In her June 25, 2014 monthly message to the world, the Blessed Mother announced that she would continue to appear as long as God wants her to. These apparitions have been going on now for thirty-three years. The Blessed Mother's apparitions in Medjugorje are the longest lasting apparitions since the Blessed Mother has been appearing on earth.

On August 25, 2014, the Blessed Mother sent an urgent message for all of us to pray to God to prevent Satan from defeating her plans for world peace and conversion. The terrible events in the world today substantiate her warning.

Thirty days after going to Medjugorje, I ended up in Cherokee State Mental Hospital diagnosed bi-polar after a car-truck accident during a trip to Iowa. I was not injured in the accident, but I was hospitalized in Cherokee by my family. This book is about my spiritual and medical triumph over bi-polar illness. I originally wrote a hand written draft of this book in 2000. The book is about the people and things that helped me not only survive mental illness but to triumph over this bio-chemical illness.

February 24, 2013 is also a notable date because it is the date for the 2012 Academy Awards. My passions are for family and friends and justice and movies. Among the movies nominated for an academy award that year was the movie *Silver Linings Playbook*. This timely movie was nominated for eight Oscars: best movie of 2012, best director for David O. Russell, best adapted screenplay by David O. Russell, best actor for Bradley Cooper, best actress for Jennifer Lawrence, best supporting actor for Robert De Niro, and best supporting actress for Jacki Weaver. Jennifer Lawrence won for best female actress.

Silver Linings Playbook was based on the novel of the same name by Matthew Quick, a teacher who had experience working with persons with mental health issues. Bradley Cooper plays Pat Salitano, a man living with great difficulty with bi-polar illness.

The movie is important to me because as I told you, in 1988 I was diagnosed with bi-polar illness and I have lived with this illness for twenty-seven years so the movie portrayal of bi-polar illness and recovery moved me deeply.

Silver Linings Playbook was nominated for four Golden Globes with Jennifer Lawrence winning for best actress. It was nominated for three

Sundance and Cherokee Moon

BAFTA awards (British Academy of Film and Television Arts) where Russell won for best adapted screenplay; four nominations from the Screen Actors Guild with Lawrence winning for best actress; nominated for five Independent Spirit Awards winning in four categories: best film, best director, best adapted screenplay and again for best actress Jennifer Lawrence.

I go into such detail about the awards this movie has received because this movie is about a still taboo subject, mental illness, but it portrays that illness with the hope of living with it and surviving it. The main character Pat Salitano, brilliantly played by Bradley Cooper, has just been released from a mental hospital with a diagnosis of bi-polar disorder. He has lost everything, it seems,--his job, his wife, his home--when he is released to live with his parents played by Robert De Niro and Jacki Weaver.

Shortly, he is introduced to a young widow and sex addict played by Jennifer Lawrence. They enter into an agreement. She will help him get his wife back if he agrees to train with her for a dance contest. He agrees. He becomes compliant (a psychiatric term meaning he takes his medicine and goes to his psychiatrist) and he and the young woman both change their lives through the discipline of dance and their budding relationship.

The ending is thrilling as they perform at the contest and love triumphs. I saw the movie twice in the theater and four times after I ordered the DVD to add to my DVD collection of mental health movies. I have bought copies of *Silver Linings Playbook* for family and friends. These movies in my collection include: *A Beautiful Mind* (with Russell Crowe as Nobel Memorial Prize in Economics winner John Nash who suffers from Schizophrenia); *Girl Interrupted* (about four young women in a mental hospital with Angelina Jolie playing a sociopath and Whoopie Goldberg playing a psychiatric nurse); *One Flew Over the Cuckoo's Nest* (with Jack Nicholson playing Randle McMurphy who is forced to take shock treatments); and *Michael Clayton* (with Tom Wilkinson playing a bi-polar lawyer Arthur Edens watched over by George Clooney playing Michael Clayton, a fixer in their New York law firm).

Michael Clayton is a legal thriller where after Edens's murder, Clayton learns that although Arthur Edens had a bizarre bi-polar episode including taking off all his clothes during a deposition, he was on to illegal conduct by the firm's client and that knowledge resulted in his murder by the client. The film discusses the law of mental health commitment when the firm

12

wants to commit Arthur. It turns out the expert in mental health commitment law in the firm is Arthur Edens himself.

(My twin daughters Mary Kay and Elizabeth have both seen this movie too and they tell me I am Arthur Edens, the bi-polar lawyer who is expert in mental commitment law. Having lived through my episodes, they tell me they can't see the movie again. I never took all my clothes off like Arthur Edens, but I did give most of my clothes away in a manic episode.)

(Wiki-pedia lists eleven modern movies and two television series including the series *Homeland* and *Black Box* where the main characters are bi-polar. Movies dealing with all mental illnesses are legion. Mental illness movies can bring big bucks to Hollywood. *A Beautiful Mind* grossed over $300 million world-wide. In 2013 it was reported that in the U.S., *Silver Linings Playbook* grossed over $132,092,000.00 and an additional $236,502,599.00 world-wide. Some of these movies, but not all, have taken mental illness out of the shadows. But even so, the stigma felt by persons with mental illness is still too prevalent today. The National Institute of Mental Illness has a far reaching anti-stigma program, and the need for this program is still great.)

Before the February 24, 2013, Academy Awards show, Katie Couric, on her *Katie* talk show on ABC, had Bradley Cooper, Robert De Niro, and writer-director David O. Russell on the show. Sidney Pollack (writer, actor, director including *Out of Africa* with Meryl Streep and Robert Redford and director of *Tootsie* with Dustin Hoffman and with Pollack in a cameo role) gave David Russell the novel *Silver Linings Playbook*, authored by Matthew Quick, six months before his, Pollack's, death.

Russell explained that he was immediately drawn to the fact-based novel because his own young adult son lives with bi-polar illness. For Russell writing the screenplay and directing the movie were a labor of love. Bradley Cooper told how he relied on a friend's experience and the advice of the younger Russell to prepare for the role. Young Russell played a part in the movie as the inquisitive teenage neighbor with a camera trying to take pictures of Pat Salitano in one of his episodes.

It was clear that the movie was personal to all of them, including Robert De Niro whose face streamed with tears during part of the discussion. Former Congressman Patrick Kennedy was on the show. Kennedy who with his father, the late U.S. Senator Ted Kennedy, spearheaded the passage of the Mental Health Parity Act mandating that insurance companies treat mental illnesses, which are scientifically documented brain chemistry illnesses, the same as other body illnesses.

I mention **Silver Linings Playbook** for several reasons. First, as I noted, is because in November of 1988, I was diagnosed with bi-polar illness (also known as "M.D." or manic-depressive illness) after a car-truck accident in Iowa when I was forty-six years old and afterward hospitalized by my family at Cherokee State Mental Hospital in Cherokee, Iowa. I was living in Omaha, NE where I lived most of my life.

A month earlier, I had taken my now late mother to Medjugorje. My new spiritual journey began six years before our October, 1988 "pilgrimage" to Medjugorje. My new spiritual journey began in late 1982, after I was in a state of profound grief and depression due to the deaths of three close male friends, two Omaha lawyer friends Benjamin Wall and Art O'Leary, both my mentors, and Dave Liddell from Denver, Colorado, a financial planner, friend and godfather to one of my daughters.

The themes of the book, Robert Redford, movies, Medjugorje, miracles and mania, run through my life even today. Let me take you with me on my spiritual and emotional journey, and triumph over bi-polar illness.

I started 1988 by attending the January Sundance Film Festival in Utah followed eight months later seeing the sun dance, the Miracle of the Sun in Medjugorje. Between these two events, as a lawyer, I settled a number of cases and handled a difficult six week discrimination trial. Finally, as I have noted, I ended up in Cherokee State Mental Hospital in Cherokee, Iowa, in November, thirty days after going to Medjugorje.

In Cherokee, I pleaded with God: "Who goes to Medjugorje and ends up thirty days later in a state mental hospital?" After days of prayer, I thought I found the answer. God took me up on my 1982 gift to Him of the rest of my life to do what He wanted with me.

Back in 1982 being profoundly grief stricken, depressed and seriously ill, I continued my daily prayers for four of my friends and others with mental illness and prayed for my family and all my friends and clients. I accepted as my new spiritual vocation prayer and living my life with bi-polar illness. For the rest of my life, I will be on various medications and seeing a psychiatrist every three months unless I live long enough to see a cure for

14

mental illness through the genome, genetic surgery or other medical advances. Bi-polar illness is an inherited illness.

The rest of my book is about my life as a mother, grandmother, friend, spiritual person, patient, author, attorney, political activist, passionate film goer and about my seven hospitalizations for bi-polar illness in twenty-six years. Three of these hospitalizations were in three different hospitals in a four week period. Two of them were in the same mental hospital thirteen years apart at Cherokee.

I join my voice with national advocates for the reform of mental hospitals and treatment and for adequate funding of mental health programs, especially community based programs, advocating through NAMI (the National Alliance on Mental Illness) and by advocating at the Nebraska legislature and with the members of Congress and in the courts. Government and private insurance funding has been slashed for mental health care. State hospitals have been closed.

Private hospitals close because of inadequate reimbursement from the federal government and the State governments. Under the Affordable Health Care Act, affectionately called Obama Care, as of July, 2013, insurance companies have to treat mental illnesses the same as other physical illnesses and also under the Mental Health Parity Act. But twenty-six states have opted out of the Medicaid expansion feature of the Affordable Care Act by not establishing State Exchanges. That provision in the law would help millions of people to have medical care including people with mental illness.

Our jails and prisons, which are usually fully funded, are the new mental hospitals due to the funding cuts in mental health care. See *Crazy: A Father's Search through America's Mental Health Madness*, by Pulitzer Prize winner Pete Early about this national scandal and his own son's experiences.

It takes courage for me to write this book about the nightmare events in my life with mental illness. It takes courage for me to write about my spiritual experiences too. Since 1988, I have mainly been a private person. My hope is that by writing about my own mental health and spiritual experiences I can give hope to other people, their families and their friends. Now more and more people are talking about their mental illnesses and more and more people are being open about their spiritual experiences.

This is the right time for me to go public. I want to help others, to be a beacon of hope and love to others who suffer mental illnesses, especially the young people, and their families and friends. I have told young people close to me that in their lifetime there will be a cure for mental illnesses through all the genome, genetic surgery and brain research. Recent articles in the New York Times have highlighted some of this exciting and dramatic research. There may even be a day in the not so distant future where non-drug treatments will not only cure mental illness but many other serious illnesses.

One of those pioneers in the field of mental illness is Dr. Karl Deisseroth, M.D., Ph.D. at Stanford University in California. He is a board certified and practicing psychiatrist treating patients and a neuroscientist doing ground breaking research called optogenetics or the use of light to turn off cells in the brain to treat and cure mental illness. When I read that Dr. Deisseroth is motivated in his research by the suffering of his patients and by the terrible side effects of psychiatric drugs some even causing suicide, my eyes filled with tears. When I told my own psychiatrist Dr. A. Mohammed Mirza, M.D. about Dr. Deisseroth's research, he put his head slightly down and I could see a tear in his eye.

Dr. Deisseroth has trained other neuroscientist in his lab and they have gone on to get funding and establish their own labs working in optogenetics. So far they have been lighting animal brains. The next step in their research is to work on donated human brains, and after that there will be trials on the brains of living human beings. If I am alive then, I want to be a volunteer subject in his research.

There is other exciting research being done manipulating the vagus nerve to cure major illnesses including Parkinson's and Diabetes by non-drug treatment. I hope to live to see the day that all these non-drug treatments are standard medical treatment. I am also diabetic.

I borrowed courage to write about my bi-polar illness from three national leaders in the field of mental health. The first national leader is Kay Redfield Jamison, Ph.D., a professor of Psychiatry at John Hopkins Medical School and author of her 1995 memoir about her own bi-polar illness titled *An Unquiet Mind: About Moods and Madness.* She has written four other books on mental illness and co-wrote *Manic Depressive*

16

Sundance and Cherokee Moon

Illness with Frederick K. Goodwin in 1990 and republished in 2007, a definitive text book on manic depressive illness.

The first mental health autobiography I read was Patty Duke's courageous memoir *A Brilliant Madness: Living with Bi-Polar Illness*, which I read with great difficulty at Cherokee State Mental Hospital in 1988 because I had trouble focusing my eyes. The book was in the library of the hospital (the only mental hospital I was in that had a library and a recreation area). Kay Redfield Jamison mentioned this same difficulty with her eyes after she was diagnosed. I am not sure if it is from the medications or part of the illness. Several months later, it went away.

Patty Duke was recently in Omaha, NE in 2014 as a speaker after a showing of her award winning movie *The Miracle Worker* where she played the young Helen Keller who was blind and deaf but achieved greatness in her life. Patty has been travelling all over the country with this classic movie. I got to thank her for giving me the courage to live with bi-polar illness through her memoir and I got to pay tribute to her in a letter thanking her published by the Omaha World Herald Newspaper. In the letter I mentioned that I pay tribute to Patty Duke for helping me through her book

Originally my friend and famous fellow author Patty McGill Smith (Her book *You Are Not Alone* is now being finished for publication) and I were to go to the event with Patty Duke but we were not able to go. I couldn't get there from Lees Summit, MO, where I now live. Patty Smith has time conflict. Our friends Nan and Ann went for us. Nan was the second person in line for autographs from Patty Duke. Nan had bought a Patty Duke recording years ago as a teenager. Patty Duke signed her record, signed a copy of my Omaha World Herald letter to the editor after reading it, and signed the program and one of the tickets to the event. Nan unselfishly gave me everything but the record, her cherished record.

Patty Duke has in the past and continues to this day to travel all over America advocating for recovery for people with mental illness while telling her own story, and years ago she was in Omaha to speak about this at a fundraising dinner for Community Alliance, a program that provides housing and treatment for people with mental illness. Patty Duke was a famous movie star when she was diagnosed in 1982 with bi-polar illness. She took an incredible career risk in writing about her own illness and recovery.

The third national leader is Ellen R. Saks, lawyer and professor of mental health law, criminal law and children and the law at the University of Southern California Law School. She wrote about living with schizophrenia in her memoir *The Center Cannot Hold: My Journey with Madness*.

Both Kay Redfield Jamison, Ph.D., professor of psychiatry at John Hopkins, and Ellen R. Saks, J.D., professor of law at the University of Southern Law School, were awarded McArthur Genius Awards and both participated in the *Charlie Rose "Brain Series"* on PBS (Public Broadcasting System) with Dr. Erick Kanter, M.D. in the Mental Health segment. The lectures and interviews of both these women can be found on Google or searched by their names, and their joint interview with Charlie Rose's PBS television show can be searched on Google or searched at *Charlie Rose "Brain Series."* All of Charlie Rose's shows can be accessed through Google or other search engines. Kay Redfield Jamison and Ellen Saks were also featured national TED lecturers.

There are excellent books by other brilliant women who share bi-polar illness with me in addition to authors Kay Redfield Jamison, Ph.D. and Ellen Saks, J.D. and Patty Duke. Carrie Fischer wrote and performed her one woman show based on her book of the same name *Wishful Drinking* about her mental illness, and her book about her life with shock treatment for her bi-polar illness and depression titled *Shockaholic*. She uses comedy in telling her story.

Two more talented women authors who have written books about their lives with bi-polar illnesses are Marya Hornbacher, a journalist and author who titled her memoir *Madness: A Bi-Polar Life*. Marya's book reads like a compelling mystery where you can't put it down because you want to see if she ever gets the message that medication is essential to wellness in most cases. A number of suicide attempts, a divorce and finally compliance and writing about her life have her now as a university professor in English.

Marya was nominated for the Pulitzer Prize for her earlier memoir *Wasted: A Memoir of Anorexia, Me and Bulimia*. I bought this book too, but as a one time sufferer of bulimia, I found the book too painful to read.

Sundance and Cherokee Moon

Finally, is the book *Marbles, Mania, Depression, Michelangelo, and Me* by talented cartoonist Ellen Forney about her life with bi-polar illness told in cartoons. All of these authors are on Google and other search engines even with interviews, blogs and websites.

My book is distinguished from the others because I talk about both my bi-polar illness and my spiritual journey and experiences before, during and after my diagnosis. My spirituality was one important element in my recovery along with family, friends, good doctors, good medications, a passion for my justice work and a passion for movies.

I bought a book after being hospitalized and diagnosed with bi-polar illness written by a Christian psychiatrist. The title was something like: *When Jesus Comes Again He Will Be Committed.* I still have that book somewhere in storage. "And who is your father?" a psychiatrist might ask.

Too often, genuine spiritual experiences are categorized as delusions and hallucinations. I was first called a religious fanatic in November, 1988, by an admitted atheist psychiatrist from India at Cherokee State Mental Hospital because of my spiritual experiences, my devotion as a Catholic and the devotion of my parents. He said the religious experiences of people in India are all forms of mass hysteria.

These extraordinary spiritual experiences of mine started one month before my mother and I went on our pilgrimage to Medjugorje and continued during our trip and for six years after our trip to Medjugorje. It was also suggested that I was schizo-affective—one who sees and hears things, because of a vision I had, and seeing the Miracle of the Sun in Medjugorje and in the United States (which I still can see).

Five years later I was given a battery of psychological tests by Omaha psychologist Joseph Stankus, Ph.D. when I was referred to him by my then psychiatrist Jack Wisman, M.D. I had met Dr. Wisman when I attended Unity Church in Omaha for a couple of years. These tests, including the MMPI or Minnesota Multi-Phasic Personality Inventory, showed that my ongoing spiritual experiences were genuine. I was on lithium at the time I took the tests. If my experiences with inner speaking or inner locutions from the Lord and my experiences with visions and automatic writing had been hallucinations, the lithium would have stopped them. It didn't because they were real.

Sundance and Cherokee Moon

I can still see the Miracle of the Sun which is one of the spiritual signs in Medjugorje as could my mother until her death seven years ago; and my spiritual experiences have sustained me through a sometime difficult life with mental illness. I will be happy to take the same battery of psychological tests again. But I only had inner locutions or inner speaking for six years.

I got the idea to take these psychological tests from the visionaries in Medjugorje because the Communist officials in Yugoslavia forced all six young visionaries take neurological and psychological tests. These tests proved that their visions were not delusions or caused by neurological disorders.

Recently I read an online article published in the British *Guardian Newspaper* titled: "Hearing Voices? You Are Not Alone," from the search engine "You Are Not Alone." (Search "You Are Not Alone" and you will find an article written by my friend Patty, Patricia McGill Smith. This article has been republished millions of times internationally for years and is still available online. She is finishing her memoir titled *You Are Not Alone* about her international work on behalf of disabled children and their parents and her own daughter Jane). The *Guardian* article reported research done in the Netherland with people who hear voices.

The research supported by MRI's of the subjects showed that the majority of people hearing voices suffer them as a result of mental illness, such as Schizophrenia, while the minority have comforting spiritual guidance and support from their voices. I consider myself in the latter category. While I am bi-polar, my psychological tests showed that my spiritual experiences are genuine.

This research also supports the inner locutions of some of my spiritual friends. I only had two exterior voices or out loud hearings. One was in Medjugorje when I was awakened and asked to pray for everyone who I came to pray for (over 500 people) and the other was in St. Margaret Church in Omaha years earlier. The loud voice told four of us and not the others in attendance that: "Father Whelan is a beacon and a light to heal the nation and we are to bear witness to this fact." My inner locutions or inner hearings were internal.

You might ask: "If you were having these great spiritual experiences how can you say you suffered?" I have thought and thought about how to explain these simultaneous events. I often told the Lord that I had read THE book, *The Book of Job*, a book in the Old Testament of the Bible, and I knew that one day the suffering would stop. But a more modern comparison on how you can be close to God and still suffer is the experience of giving birth. God is the birth coach. You still have to suffer to produce the miracle of birth, but your birth coach is there helping you throughout, just as God is with us at all times.

Spiritually, as St. Therese the Little Flower of Jesus noted, joining our suffering with that of Jesus on the cross is a road to salvation. Famous psychiatrist and well published author M. Scott Peck, M.D. of *The Road Less Travelled* once wrote that we are all meant to suffer and to learn the meaning of suffering in our lives. There is a famous painting called *Footprints*. You see two sets of footprints in the sand and then just one. The one is when Jesus is carrying you.

This is probably a good time to note that the families and friends of people with mental illness suffer too. I was forty-six when I was diagnosed after that accident, but my daughters were only nineteen. My illness deeply impacted their lives. Besides having a mother who could not work, a mother who was mentally ill and under treatment, they were forced to live on their own and to support themselves and to find strength from others. I am proud to say that both Mary Kay and Elizabeth graduated from the University of Kansas in Lawrence, Kansas, and Elizabeth graduated from the University of Nebraska Law School in Lincoln, Nebraska, on their own. Like too many of our young people, they still have tremendous student loan debts to pay.

My mother also suffered for me and she suffered for years from severe depression herself only to be depression free that last three years of her life on new medication. The depression gene comes down to us from both our mother's and our father's families, from the "Irish gene," and I believe I trace my bi-polar illness from my Grandmother Green's side of the family. She had two of her eleven siblings who appear to have been mentally ill. One of my mother's sisters also suffered from mental illness.

Before I go on, I want to mention six people who also gave me courage to write about my survival with and triumph over mental illness and about my spiritual life these past twenty-six years. The first is Oprah Winfrey. I started regularly watching *Oprah* after I returned from Cherokee State Mental Hospital. I had lots of time to watch television since I could no

21

longer work and I couldn't see to read. She introduced me to so many people who had survived and triumphed over life's adversities, whether they be physical or mental illness or other tragedies. She also introduced me to Deepak Chopra, M.D., a mind-body physician and spiritual leader and author of many books, many of which I own and have read, and he is currently working with Oprah to bring the "21 Day Meditation" series on the internet to millions of people world wide.

Oprah introduced me to Larry Dossey, M.D., author of *Healing Words: The Power of Prayer and the Practice of Medicine*, copyright Larry Dossey, M.D. 1993. In his book, which I own, Dr. Dossey reported on scientific studies that proved that people who were prayed for healed faster than those not prayed for even if these people did not know they were being prayed for. He even showed the power of prayer over the growth of cells in Petrie dishes. The cells prayed over rapidly grew over the ones not prayed over. I later tell the story of how I even prayed over crops. Dr. Dossey showed that the power of prayer is universal and not necessarily related to any particular religion although it is often associated with religions. Even in my agnostic years, and I had a few of those, I still continued to pray. I intently prayed: "Oh God, if there is a God, please help me."

And I want to thank Wayne Dyer, Ph.D., a spiritual and motivational writer and speaker. I read Wayne Dyer's first book *Your Erroneous Zones* when I was a senior in law school and decided as a result to run for the Omaha City Council my last semester of law school. As a single, never married mother, there were risks, but I had good name recognition because of my late father James. F. Green, husband, father, son, lawyer, politician and public speaker. My dad, because of his beautiful baritone voice and skill as a speaker, was called another William Jennings Byron. William Jennings Bryon ran for President from Nebraska. He was noted for his speaking skills, his "Golden Throat." While I was on the Omaha City Council, Wayne Dyer came to Omaha. My friend Carol Kangior and I went to see him. The civic auditorium was filled to the ceiling with 18,000 people.

I have followed Wayne Dyer in his PBS television specials and I have bought his books and DVD's since then. I especially like the DVDs of the pilgrimage where he led 169 people to Assisi, Italy, the village where St. Francis of Assisi lived and founded his Franciscan Order and performed

22

miracles. Pope Francis of the Catholic Church took the name Francis after St. Francis, patron of the poor and animals.

Wayne Dyer then took the 169 pilgrims to Lourdes where the Blessed Mother of God appeared eighteen times to St. Bernadette and told her to dig in a spot of dirt. When Bernadette did, a stream of healing water later flowed. People from all over the world come to Lourdes to be healed by the holy waters even today.

And Wayne Dyer took his pilgrims to Medjugorje where the Blessed Mother, who calls herself Our Lady Queen of Peace, continues to appear there everyday since that first apparition on June 24, 1981. That day she appeared to six young people who have been guided to spread the messages Our Lady gives them. That DVD set is titled: *Experiencing the Miraculous:* **Assisi, Lourdes and Medjugorje.** I gave sets to three friends including the Poor Clare Sisters whose order was founded by St.Clare of Assisi a friend and follower of St. Francis.

It is my dream to take my daughter Elizabeth, who is interested, on a pilgrimage to Lourdes, France where the Blessed Mother appeared to St. Bernadette, to Lisieux, France the home of St. Therese, the Little Flower of Jesus, and to Medjugorje. Both St. Therese's and St. Bernadette's bodies are incorrupt or intact and can be seen. My friend Grace Ann Ancona got to go on this same pilgrimage June, 2014. She said that St. Therese and St. Bernadette are beautiful. It was her third trip to Medjugorje, once with her husband who was just as inspired and once alone with a group.

If we don't get to Ireland before I die, Elizabeth is going there with my life insurance money left after she buries my ashes. She says she is taking some of my ashes to Ireland and the rest will be here. We are Irish Americans. I hope when I go to Ireland while I am alive that we get to meet with the Magdalene sisters, the Irish unwed mothers imprisoned in Catholic orders of nuns and forced to give up their children, (who I write about in my book *Women of Courage: The Rights of Single Mothers and Their Children Inspired by Crystal Chambers a New Rosa Parks,* see Chapter 14) and to meet with Philomena Lee, whose story as one of the Magdalenes was documented in a book and a movie titled: 'Philomena.'

The movie 'Philomena' was nominated for an Academy Award and so was the famous British actress Judy Dench who played her. The real

23

Sundance and Cherokee Moon

Philomena Lee and the actor Steve Coogan got to meet Pope Francis. A Vatican spokesman said that the Vatican would see to it that the records of births and adoptions of the children of the Magdalenes would be released so that families can be reunited. Many of these women have died without reunification.

In the meantime Elizabeth and I have taken an arm chair pilgrimage by watching the DVDs *Therese* (about St. Therese), *Song of Bernadette* (about Lourdes where the Blessed Mother appeared to St. Bernadette), (Jennifer Jones won the Academy Award for playing St. Bernadette and so did the movie) and *Gospa* or "Mother" (with the famous actor Martin Sheen playing Father Jozo, the priest who protected the six children from the Communist government officials in the first years of the apparitions in Medjugorje). Finally we watched *The Miracle of Fatima* (about Fatima where the Blessed Mother appeared to three children and 100,000 people saw the spinning Miracle of the Sun, the Blessed Mother and St. Joseph holding the child Jesus). I obtained these movies from Amazon.

Recently, I read a book sponsored by the Fatima Society titled: *The Truth about Fatima.* The events that last day of Our Lady's apparitions to the three children in Fatima, Portugal and the 100,000 people gathered there were even more spectacular than shown in the movie. The Blessed Mother appeared with St. Joseph who was holding the baby Jesus. All could see the Holy Family. And the sun more than spun, it came to the earth and it showered the pilgrims assembled there with various colors that shone on the their faces and bodies reflecting the changing colors of the sun. Our Lady had told the three children, Lucia, Jacinta and Francisco that on her last visit on October 13, 1917 she would show the whole world who she was. Jacinta and Francisco died very young of influenza. Lucia became a nun and lived a long life. She continued to have apparitions of Our Lady and of Our Lord. They are all up for beatification and sainthood in the Catholic Church.

The Autobiography of a Soul by St. Therese is one of the spiritual books that gave me courage to write about my own spiritual experiences. My family has always been devoted to St. Therese. One of my sisters and one of my nieces are named after her and my children were born on her feast day. I first read her autobiography when I was a postulant in the Sisters of Mercy in Omaha in 1960. I felt she was my sister too.

Sundance and Cherokee Moon

I owe a debt to the late Victor Frankl, M.D. the psychiatrist who authored the internationally acclaimed book *Man's Search for Meaning.* This book is about his survival in four Nazi prison camps during World War II including Auschwitz and his creation of logotherapy. "Logo" stands for "meaning." Some of the prisoners who survived had an image of a loved one they would be reunited with. That image kept them enduring the tortures and harsh life in the camps. This belief gave meaning to their lives. Dr. Frankl's dream of seeing his wife again kept him alive. Unfortunately when the war was ended and the Americans came to free the prisoners, Dr. Frankl's search ended in the knowledge that his wife and both of his parents died in the gas chambers.

Having a purpose and meaning or "logo" in life is crucial for survival. Dr. Frankl believed also in bibliotherapy or book therapy. I too am a believer in bibliotherapy. And when I returned from the convent in 1961 I read every spiritual and psychological book I could find, including Dr. Frankl's book, to seek new meaning in my life and a new sense of purpose.

When I was pregnant with my twins in 1969, I read all the books on pregnancy and child rearing at the Cinnaminson Public Library in New Jersey when I was staying with my Aunt Jeanie and Uncle Ed Furay. My various library cards over the years and the books I checked out and bought have enriched my life.

I amassed quite a library of spiritual and self-help books in the 1990's through 2003 which I lent to my late friend Carole Barnes when I moved to Kansas City. Believing that I had given her the books, Carole gave them to an alcoholic treatment center. I pray that these books continue to help the men and women in recovery. I had failed to keep a list of these books. I wanted to share them with you. But I share a few of the ones I remember and have purchased anew.

One other spiritual book that formed my own spiritual life is *The Seven Story Mountain* by the late Trapist Monk Thomas Merton, 1948, 1998 50th Anniversary Edition. In 1980, I traveled with seven other Omahans for Peace members to a nuclear peace conference in St. Louis. During our long hours in the van, we found out that all eight of us had read Thomas Merton's *Seven Story Mountain* and had been deeply spiritually influenced by it. The conference session I attended was on accidental nuclear war. After that I met a filmmaker who was doing a documentary on accidental nuclear war. He was looking for financing to complete the film. I contacted my neighbor Warren Buffett on his behalf and Warren helped with the financing.

On July 13, 2014, CBS *60 Minutes* television show featured a story on our nuclear underground arsenal developed in the '60's with an interview with the Air Force official now in charge and the Air Force monitors who man the missile sites. Leslie Stahl was the reporter. The Air Force cooperated fully with *60 Minutes*. Also in the piece, experts were interviewed suggesting that the underground missiles are more dangerous than the missiles on our bombers and ships because the underground missiles cannot be sent back if there is an accidental release of the missiles but the ones on airplanes and ships can be retrieved. A segment of the show discussed all the accidental and near accidental bombings that have occurred since the 1960's. I learned at that peace conference and from the film maker that our real danger is from accidental nuclear bombings.

And finally I want to thank Jack Canfield, co-author with Mark Victor Hanson of the *Chicken Soup for the Soul* series and Steve Harrison of Bradley Communications for encouraging me and others to tell our stories. I was and am their continuous student. They encouraged me to tell my story and taught me how to do it. They mentored me in their Best Seller Blueprint program.

Since Oprah started her *OWN* Network, Oprah Winfrey Network, she began a Sunday series called *Super Soul Sundays.* Her guests are spiritual leaders, healers, and self-help authors and teachers. Since I go to Mass at noon on Sunday, I watch Oprah's "Super Soul Sunday" with Oprah talking with her guests at 10:00 a. m. Oprah is so inspired and inspiring. I wanted to send her a thank you letter and a copy of this book to show my gratitude to her but I was informed by a receptionist in her Los Angeles office that Oprah does not accept letters or packages apparently because of bomb threats according to this employee. Her security is tighter than the President's. You can contact her through her website Oprah.com.

After a thirteen year absence from the Catholic Church, I returned in 1982, due to the holiness of Fr. Bill Whelan a Charismatic healing priest in Omaha part of the Charismatic Renewal who was for years my spiritual director. I returned for the Mass and the Sacraments and for a spiritual community and because of the Church's activism on social justice issues. At the time I was in a severe depression triggered by grief at the loss of those three close male friends, my boss and mentor Ben Wall, my friend

26

and my daughter Elizabeth's godfather Dave Liddell and my friend and mentor Arthur O'Leary in that order, all who died in a thirty day period in the spring of 1982. I had no health insurance, and I desperately needed healing so what could I lose.

That emotional healing began with the first healing Mass of Father Bill Whelan's that I attended with my mother. My personal experience with the Catholic Church since then has been good in spite of the pedophile scandal which I abhor. Any religion that helps you fulfill the two great commandments to love God above all others and to love thy neighbor as you love yourself is good. Jesus revised that second commandment after his resurrection and stated that we must love others as he loves us. Any religion or no religion that helps you fulfill these two commandments is good. And you don't need a religion to fulfill them, but it helps.

In this book I talk about some of the holy priests in my life including Father Whelan and Father Halley and priests from both Catholic and Episcopalian Churches. I believe that in the emphasis on the horrific acts of pedophile priests the truly holy and dedicated priests are over looked. I have been blessed with holy priests from my first parish when I was a child and in kindergarten and first grade at Blessed Sacrament Parish in Omaha to my parish Our Lady of the Presentation in Lees Summit, Missouri these past several years and Sacred Heart in Omaha which I attend in Omaha when I am there.

I have of late been criticized by some for staying in the Catholic Church because of the criminal pedophile scandal and cover up. My answer for staying is the statement I made to my former pastor here in Lees Summit Father Michael Cleary after it became known that our bishop, Bishop Robert Finn, failed to report to law enforcement the sexual abuse of young girls by a priest of the diocese. This failure caused further injury to more innocent young girls and the Bishop was convicted of failing to report. On April 21, 2015, Pope Francis accepted Bishop Finn's resignation. He was apparently given this option rather than removal.

I told Father: "Father, the corruption in the Catholic Church from this pedophile scandal goes all the way up to the Vatican. If the Catholic Church survives, it will be because of holy priests like you, Father." And lay people, I would add. The Church is nothing without us lay people. And the healing of the Church is being led by our new Pope Francis.

Sundance and Cherokee Moon

Another response I have given to critics is: "I want to be part of the revolution, the reformation of the Catholic Church." Our lovable new Pope Francis, America's *Time Magazine's* **"Man of the Year,"** is leading the Church reformation by bringing the Cardinals and Bishops back to humility and back to its roots of love, forgiveness, mercy and caring for the poor and the vulnerable and by his recent synod or meeting of Cardinals. I love this Pope, but I pray that he has the time and the health to lead the church regarding the reform including issues of women in the Church and women Priests. The vocations of these 600 plus duly ordained and excommunicated by Pope Benedict XVI women priests come from the same Lord who calls men to the priesthood, who called Pope Francis to the priesthood. I also pray that the greater church changes its attitude about Gay, Lesbian, Transgender and Bi-sexual individuals who are created by God just like the rest of us are and gay marriage and about single mothers.

Pope Francis welcomes all people in the Church and like Jesus, loves all people. He is called the Pope of the world. The last pope, Pope Benedict XVI, was steering the Church to only a conservative Church and excluding others who are moderate and liberal like me and many of my friends. God Bless Pope Francis and may he have a long, safe and healthy life. I wrote this paragraph well before Pope Francis exclaimed he had but two or three years. We need him longer than that. Pray for his healing.

Pope Francis recently took responsibility for the acts of the pedophile priests and asked the victims for forgiveness. This is the first time a Pope has acknowledged the culpability of the church in this scandal. More needs to be done, however. I understand that the Pope is reviewing the files of three bishops who are accused of complicity over the pedophile scandals. One is Bishop Robert Finn. This is just a drop in the bucket. What about the Cardinals like Cardinal Bernard Law of Boston who was given exile in Rome with a Basilica of his own by Pope John Paul II and other cardinals in the world.

We Catholics here in America are still chaffing over the sanctuary given by John Paul II to Cardinal Law of that scandal ridden Boston Archdiocese. The cover up of pedophile priests by Cardinal Law stands out as one of the worst scandals in the American Church, but not the only one. The diocese of Philadelphia and Los Angeles are two more of the worst. The Cardinal in Philadelphia, who kept two sets of books, one for pedophile priests and one for holy priests, died of a heart attack before he could be prosecuted.

Sundance and Cherokee Moon

Memorial Day weekend 2014, Pope Francis led a pilgrimage of prayer for all peoples to Israel and Palestine where in ceremonies he sought reconciliation with the Orthodox religions and the Jewish and Muslim communities. The Pope's pilgrimage was televised worldwide. Pope Francis ended his pilgrimage to the Holy Lands by inviting the Jewish and Palestinian leaders to the Vatican to pray together for peace and harmony in the Middle East. Leaders from both sides accepted his invitation and came to the Vatican in Rome, Italy. The prayers of millions of people for how many years will be required to see peace there.

It was announced as of late 2014 that the Pope is coming to America to Philadelphia, Pennsylvania to the World Family Conference, to speak to the Congress in Washington, D.C. and to New York City to speak at the United Nations all in 2015. There is much anticipation here in America among Catholics and others about the Pope's 2015 visit here.

I am an American Catholic, one who by my professional oath as an attorney, and my personal commitment, supports the United States Constitution, especially freedom of speech and equal protection for all. The First Amendment Freedom of Speech Clause and Fourteenth Amendment Equal Protection Clause are not always honored by the hierarchy of the Catholic Church or many other churches including the Mormons. Part of that First Amendment also protects religious freedom of the various religions, some of which ironically don't believe in freedom of speech and equal protection for all.

Take note of the excommunication of the 600 duly ordained women Catholic priests and the recent excommunication of the Mormon woman active in the movement for women priests in the Mormon Church and the effort of internationally known Pastor Rick Warren, author of *The Purpose Driven Life*, and thirteen other Protestant pastors who want the government to allow them to discriminate against lesbian, gay, transgender and bi-sexual people. This is all outrageous. Some of these churches also continue to discriminate against single, unwed mothers and their children.

Like the majority of American Catholics, I support the ordination of women Catholic priests and the removal of the excommunication of the 600 plus duly ordained women Catholic priests. I support married priests, many of whom have already been accepted into the Catholic Church from Orthodox and Episcopal religions which allow married priests. I support the ninety-nine percent of Catholic women including me who have used contraceptives during our reproductive years.

I support birth control as well as the rights of gay, lesbian, bi-sexual and transgender persons to full equality. A recent New York Times/CBS poll showed the overwhelming support for these progressive issues by the majority of American Catholics. And like sixty percent of American Catholics, I voted twice for President Barack Obama. I was blessed to attend his 2008 Inauguration in Washington, D.C. I pray for Pope Francis and President Obama every day. The President has the Republican Congress thwarting him and the Pope has the Roman Curia and both of their lives are constantly being threatened.

When the Guttmacher study of Catholic women came out a few years ago, my former pastor in Kansas City gave a sermon on it and said he was just giving the facts, but that for the second time in modern times lay people in the Church were ahead of the hierarchy of the Church on a major issue. He cited the first example as the Civil Rights Movement. The Church was slow to get involved, but individual priests, nuns and lay people did. He said birth control was the second time.

Like many Catholics, I support the work of the North American nuns or sisters, and ask the Vatican to wholeheartedly praise their works and to stop limiting their excellent works for all peoples. Pope Benedict XVI started this persecution and Pope Francis has since praised the nuns but the Vatican still requires their leadership to have pre-approval for all speakers. This is not done for priests.

Recent statistics proved that effective use of birth control has dramatically reduced the number of abortions in this country back to the low level before Roe v Wade, the trimester United States Supreme Court decision on abortion. And there was a study in Maryland where free access to birth control reduced the number of abortions to 3%. Most of these women chose the I.U.D., inter-uterine device. It is our pro-choice President, President Barack Obama, who has done more to reduce the number of abortions than any other president because of the inclusion of free contraceptives in the Affordable Care Act he signed into law after the majority Democrat Congress passed it.

I also support the right of people to believe or not believe and to find their own spiritual path with or without organized religion. I have always been taught that faith is a gift from God, faith in the existence of God. Polls show that 85% of all Americans believe in God. The Blessed Mother in her appearances in Medjugorje asks everyone to pray for the conversion of all souls and for world Peace. The world desperately needs peace.

I also support a single payer government health insurance plan including low cost prescriptions for all Americans including persons with mental illness, and cancer, where prescription medications are so expensive and lack of affordable private health insurance prevents many people with mental illness from treatment and even employment. This support for a single payer health system is a moral issue with me and I continue to advocate for universal health care. In its absence, I support the Affordable Care Act which, with all the website problems worked out, provides millions of people (Republicans, Democrats and Independents and members of the U.S. Congress including Senator Ted Cruz) with comprehensive health care, over eleven million people to date. It has been called the program condemned to fail which refuses to fail. A challenge to that act is again before the U.S. Supreme Court regarding the exchanges. The decision will come down June of 2015.

But going back to *Silver Linings Playbook,* as I previously noted, the character Pat Solitano recovered from his only hospitalization and rehabilitation with the encouragement of a young woman because of whom he went back to his psychiatrist, went back on his medications and engaged in the discipline of preparing for a dance competition with her, a physically and emotionally healthy endeavor. He had loving parents as well and good friends. It should be noted that evidence proves that exercise, and dancing is exercise, reduces depression. I am proud that the original study demonstrating this fact was done at the University of Nebraska. Nebraska has been my home for most of my life.

While Pat Solitano and I share the same biochemical brain chemistry illness called bi-polar illness, it took more that one hospitalization for me. My ups and downs resulted in seven hospitalizations, different medications and a number of psychiatrists. I survived with the help of these psychiatrists, the prayers and support of two holy Charismatic healing priests, Father William "Bill" Whelan and Father Thomas Halley, S.J., and a cloistered order of nuns, the Poor Clare Sisters of Omaha, Nebraska. I was asked by three of the Poor Clare Sisters in the mid l990s to join their order at the funeral of Sister Mary Rock knowing I was a single mother and after I was diagnosed with bi-polar illness. I gave it prayerful thought but decided my vocation is in the world.

I was helped by great physicians like Michael Sorrell, M.D. (the University of Nebraska Medical School is now the Michael Sorrel University of Nebraska Medical School), Robert Bowman, M.D., James Morgan, M.D. of Omaha and Alan Salkind, M.D., Shadrach Smith, M.D., Dorota Walewicz, M.D. and Nurbani Parini, M.D. here in Kansas City who all treated my physical illnesses without attributing them to my psychiatric diagnosis, i.e., not treating me as a mental case. I have nine distinct medical conditions including bi-polar illness and diabetes with seven of these conditions treated with medications. I consider myself well. I treasure the love of my friends and a family that truly loved me and took actions to protect me that I didn't always like at the time for which I am grateful.

I love my family for everything they did to protect me and I know that they only did what they did out of love. One of my siblings recently told me she felt so helpless not knowing how to help me. I pray that my book will be of help to families as well as people suffering mental illness or any illness. Spending quality time is one way to help and protecting your loved ones is another way to help. There is a fine line between needing protection and needing independence.

I want my siblings to know that I appreciate everything they did to protect me. If it had been one of them who needed protection, I would have been of help. I thank you Pat, Therese, Jane, John, Margie, Liz and Alice and their spouses.

Two of those seven hospitalizations were in the same hospital, Cherokee State Mental Hospital in Cherokee, Iowa, thirteen years apart; three hospitalizations were in three different hospitals in a four week period in early 2001: Immanuel in Omaha, Mercy in Council Bluffs, Iowa and Cherokee State Mental Hospital in Cherokee, Iowa. These later hospitalizations were the result of a failed 1989 stomach stapling surgery that caused me to constantly vomit my food and my medications. Three years ago a scientific journal reported that stomach stapling surgery failed with persons with bi-polar illness. They didn't know why.

My last hospitalization was under the care of my much beloved psychiatrist Dr. A. Mohammed Mirza, M.D. in a two week voluntary and

32

excellent day program in 2005 at Two Rivers Mental Hospital in Kansas City, Missouri. Dr. Mirza had me enter the program to adjust the dosage of my new medication Geodon, a drug that, along with an older drug Lamictal, gave me back a normal life. I was writing my book *Women of Courage* and had become obsessed with writing it and manic. My daughter Elizabeth, my sister Therese and her husband Paul Bigelow held an intervention for me. I told them that I trusted Dr. Mirza and if he thought I was manic, I would follow his direction. He increased the dosage of my Geodon medication and had me voluntarily enter a day program in Kansas City called Two Rivers where he could see me daily and monitor the effect of Geodon. It was a terrific therapeutic program.

Since 2005, I have normal highs and lows, not mania and depression. I am grateful to Dr. Mirza and to the women and men who created Geodon and Lamictal. My bariatric physician in Kansas City, MO, Dr. Shadrach Smith, M.D. asked me to go to my psychiatrist and other doctors to change my medications to medications that did not cause weight gain. I was on Lithium which caused me to have weight gain and kidney disease. Geodon does not cause weight gain and I have no side effects from this new drug or from Lamictal.

Since 1988, I have lived in five cities in three states: Omaha, Nebraska; Lenexa and Overland Park, Kansas; Kansas City, Missouri and for the last five years, I have been living happily in Lees Summit, Missouri, a bedroom community of Kansas City. In Lee Summit, I have been handling law cases remotely in Omaha because all court filings including evidence and briefs are through the internet and mediating cases in Nebraska, Kansas and Missouri with the EEOC here and writing this book. I retired from the private practice of law January, 2015. I want to devote more of my time to writing.

It was a long and sometimes rocky road to become mentally well. And my spirituality was an important key to my survival and wellness.

In this book I want to share my spiritual journey with bi-polar illness with you. As a writer, I maintain that the ups and downs of my journey are equally dramatic. I share with you because I want to help other people living with mental illness, their families and friends, their doctors, people struggling with emotional and physical illnesses and the general public. I want to help bury the stigma of mental illness. I want to share the hope and love I was given. There are over 60 million people in the United

States and 380 million people in the world who suffer from some form of mental illness.

My spiritual experiences before and with bi-polar illness may have been unique for me but not for the other people who have gone to Medjugorje or other people who have had deep spiritual or mystical experiences unrelated to Medjugorje. The very popular *Chicken Soup for the Soul* series of books created by my mentor Jack Canfield and his partner Mark Victor Hansen, often working with various co-authors, is one series of books with people telling about their spiritual experiences. I especially treasure *Chicken Soup for the Soul: A Book of Miracles* by Jack Canfield, Mark Victor Hansen and LeAnn Thieman and *Chicken Soup for the Soul: Miracles from Heaven* by Jack Canfield, Mark Victor Hanson and Amy Newmar. These books record the special spiritual experiences of everyday people like me as do *The Hot Chocolate for the Mystical Soul series* of books by Arielle Ford. The *Hot Chocolate* series should be reprinted.

My favorite story is in the original *Hot Chocolate for the Mystical Soul* book at page 70 by Bruce Stephen Holms titled "A Window Washer, a Woman with a Baby, and a Gift." The former window washer Morris Forte was on Mr. Holms' show on Timeless Voyager Radio. The woman with a baby was the Blessed Mother who was always carrying the baby Jesus. She came to him repeatedly meeting him on the steps of St. Patrick's Cathedral, at a coffee shop, and in his apartment through the walls always asking him to pray with her and telling him that she had a gift for him. When he finally realized who she was, she told him that she was giving him the gift of extra sensory perception and that he could only use it for good. The adult Jesus also appeared to him too. Morris Forte became known world wide for his gift and helped thousands of people with it. What a wonderful way to help people heal. God used Morris for good.

These recorded spiritual experiences are universal for people of all faiths or no faith and there is modern research documenting the importance of spirituality in healing mental illness. In an article titled "Benefits of Spirituality Affirmed" by Katrina Gay, NAMI Director of Communications (National Alliance on Mental Illness) in the winter 2013 edition of the *NAMI Advocate*, a report is cited of a study on the role of spirituality and health published in the Journal of Religion and Health captioned "Relationships among Spirituality, Religious Practices, Personality Factors, and Health for Five Different Faiths." An abstract of that study, which mirrored the research conducted by NAMI associates,

Sundance and Cherokee Moon

can be found at www.ncbi.nlm.nih.gov/pubmed/22618413. To learn more about spirituality and recovery see www.nami.org/faithnet.

BOOK I: SUNDANCE AND MEDJUGORJE 1988

CHAPTER I: ROBERT REDFORD AND THE SUNDANCE FILM FESTIVAL

Let me go on with my story. I chose the title of this book because the word "Sundance" represents the Sundance Film Institute and the Sundance Film Festival started by Robert Redford. "Sundance" came from the name of the Sundance Kid character played by Robert Redford in the movie *Butch Cassidy and the Sundance Kid* with Paul Newman as Butch Cassidy.

Thousands of people have attended this festival since 1984. And in my book, "Sundance" also stands for the Sun Dance or Miracle of the Sun in Medjugorje. Over forty million people, or pilgrims as we are called, have traveled to Medjugorje since June 24, 1981. Millions of them have seen the Miracle of the Sun and other spiritual phenomena.

The word "Cherokee" is used because of my hospitalizations in 1988 and 2001 at Cherokee State Mental Hospital in Cherokee, Iowa. The word "Moon" is used in contrast to the sun to reflect the brightness of mania contrasted to the dark night of depression.

In January, 1988, I went to the Sundance Film Festival, handled some civil rights cases, took my mother to Medjugorje in October, and thirty days later after a car-truck accident in November, I ended up in Cherokee State Mental Hospital in Cherokee, Iowa, diagnosed with bi-polar illness.

Going back to 1977, professionally I was sworn in as a Nebraska attorney in a ceremony with my classmates and other law graduates before the Nebraska Supreme Court on September 13, 1977. That previous May, I graduated from Creighton University Law School in Omaha, Nebraska, and simultaneously took an oath of office as one of seven elected Omaha City Council Members out of seventy-one candidates. My younger brother John Green attended all my appearances for me during the general election while I was studying for and taking my final exams to graduate.

I came in fourth and was the only woman elected that year to the Omaha City Council in Omaha, Nebraska. I was the third woman ever elected to the Omaha City Council. Other women have been elected to the City Council since then including my classmate Brenda Council. And in May, 2013, a Republican woman was elected Mayor, the first woman mayor and the third woman who ran for Mayor of the city. Jim Suttle, the Mayor she defeated, was a good mayor who brought much success to Omaha. Hopefully she will be good for Omaha, too.

Skipping forward, in December of 1987, I received my half share of a $54,000.00 court awarded attorney fee in the successful trial for my client Rudy Avila against the City of Omaha for discrimination against him for being Hispanic. Attorney Alan Kirshen agreed to be lead attorney to my second chair for the trial part. He questioned Mr. Avila and all the witnesses while I kept a handwritten transcript of the trial for appeal if necessary and made sure all the exhibits were introduced and received. I had represented Mr. Avila for five years on this case before we got a 90 Day Right to Sue Letter from the EEOC, the U.S. Equal Employment Opportunity Commission, allowing us to go into federal court to try his case. The law has since been changed. You can get a Right to Sue Letter 180 days after filing your charge or earlier if the EEOC is not able to complete its investigation by then. They have six months to complete their investigation.

The attorney fee award by the judge was one of the largest attorney fee awards for a civil rights case in the U.S. District Court for Nebraska at that time. For years, judges were awarding low attorney fees in civil rights cases as they did in environmental cases nationwide. The belief was that they did so to discourage attorneys from taking these cases. From what I understand this has become a problem again especially in the 8th Circuit covering Nebraska, Iowa, Missouri and other states. The 8th Circuit appears to be hostile to civil rights cases.

Also in 1987, I bought a copy of an American Film Institute book. The book pictured Humphrey Bogart and Katherine Hepburn on the cover in their period costumes for the movie *African Queen.* What attracted me to the book, besides the cover, were the schedules inside and all the contact information for film festivals in the United States and their dates. On the list was the U.S.A. Film Festival sponsored by Robert Redford's Sundance

Sundance and Cherokee Moon

Film Institute. For many years since then, it has been called the Sundance Film Festival. I refer to it as the Sundance Film Festival.

Six years earlier in 1981, I watched an hour long special on Robert Redford and his Sundance Film Institute on PBS, Public Broadcasting System, a public television network. The best part of the special was the interview with Robert Redford, Hollywood actor and director and founder of Sundance. He talked about his love for movies and movie making that started in his childhood in Los Angeles, California. His passion for movies from childhood on reminded me of the early childhood passion for movies of Francois Truffaut, the famous French film director and actor, expressed in his autobiography *The Films of My Life*.

I felt the same tremendous connection to Robert Redford in that interview as I did to Francois Truffaut when I read his autobiography. Like Truffaut, at age five, I too fell in love with movies. We lived six houses from the Minne Lusa Movie Theater in the Florence area of Omaha, and that's where I fell in love with movies. That romance has stayed with me all through my life, good times and bad. While I will never be a director and actor like Redford and Truffaut, I am one of the most important elements of the movie industry, a passionate movie goer.

When I got my fee in Rudy Avila's case in late 1987, I contacted the Sundance Institute to make reservations to attend the 1988 festival. That year, the festival ran from January 15th through the 24th. My birthday is the 17th of January. I decided I would give myself a wonderful birthday present. My late father James F. Green always taught us that we should give ourselves a birthday present too. This was the first time I followed his advice.

I was told by a woman on the phone at Sundance that I could purchase a universal pass for the festival for the first week or the second week or for both weeks. The pass would get me into any movie I wanted to see and to all of the night time parties sponsored by each of the festival's individual sponsors from the industry or other corporate sponsors such as AT&.T that year.

No way was I going to go for one week. I sent in the money for the entire two weeks. I was told to fly into Salt Lake City and that staff from the festival would meet me and any other festival goers at the airport to give us rides up the mountains to Park City where the festival was held. I made a reservation to stay at a motel with a pool and a gym. It turned out that the motel had a theater in it and it was one of the sites for movies and for the film workshops during the festival.

Just as I had been told, there were people with festival signs at the Salt Lake City airport. I checked in with them and got my suitcase, and with a few others rode up to Park City in a van with festival staff. It was snowing up in the mountains. The ride up was beautiful. On the way up we were informed that we had to be ready by six o'clock to ride down to the opening premiere in Salt Lake City.

Going up to Park City, I met a woman in the van named Louise Levison from Los Angeles. She was in film financing. We rode back together and sat together at the theater in Salt Lake City. We would become fast friends during the two weeks. I have a picture of Louise and Me along with a man from the Austin, TX, Film Festival. Hopefully it will upload to in back of this book. The photograph was taken by Sandra Miller, a festival photographer.

I bought a special automatic camera back in Omaha. I wanted to get good pictures of Robert Redford and to take pictures of the festival. Louise and I sat eight rows from the stage and directly in front of Robert Redford. I took four pictures of him only to find out when the pictures were developed that all that showed up was the bald head of the man a few rows ahead of us. Redford was just a dot.

Robert Redford was the host of the premiere and of the entire festival. If the audience wasn't already excited about being there like I was, Robert Redford's speech opening the festival had to excite them. After welcoming us, he introduced director Louis Malle. Malle's film *Au Revoir Les Enfants* (Goodbye the Children) was the movie premiered that night. There would be other premieres. The film was based on Malle's own childhood experiences in a Catholic boarding school in German occupied France. The nuns were hiding Jewish children in the school. The Germans discovered the Jewish children and took them away. The ending was devastating. Malle's wife, the American actress Candace Bergen, joined him in the festivities.

The post premiere party was held back at a hall in Park City. "At last," I thought, "I will finally get to meet Robert Redford." I was standing by myself watching all the other people at the party, including the film critic

Sundance and Cherokee Moon

Leonard Maltin (seen regularly on television), when a young woman came toward me and said: "I don't know what to do. He's stuck in the stair well."

She explained to me that Robert Redford was suffering a panic attack and was stuck in the stair well since arriving at the party. "What will everyone think?" she pleaded. "They will understand," I replied. The young woman introduced herself. She was one of Robert Redford's secretaries. She was so concerned about him that she walked up to me, a stranger, to express her concern. All I could offer her was compassion for Robert Redford and for her.

I went back to the motel later that night and gave myself a talk. I realized I took my favorite movie actors and actresses and people in the entertainment world for granted when just like me they are human, they are vulnerable human beings. They give us so much pleasure with their talents and what do we give back other than the price of a movie ticket I asked myself. So I decided right then and there that I would start praying for people in the entertainment industry starting with Robert Redford, Elizabeth Taylor and my other favorite stars. I would especially pray for them all during the half hour or so before a movie started. I did this for years and now I include them in the "friend" section of my daily prayers.

While Robert Redford and Elizabeth Taylor were my favorite movie stars, I also had as favorites Kathryn Hepburn and Spencer Tracy. I think I have seen most of their movies on television and in the theaters. Kathryn Hepburn was my role model.

Park City could have been built as a movie set it is so charming. With the snow coming down all the time. Park City reminded me of the classic movie *White Christmas* with Bing Crosby and Rosemary Clooney. Here you could see skiers going up and down the mountains day and night, and the streets below were filled with movie goers. Just as you could watch the skiers going up and down the mountains day and night, you could see lines of movies goers at the various theaters day and night visiting with each other while waiting their turns to see the movies.

There are certain movies that become annual treats. Before Thanksgiving, 2013, my then eleven year old granddaughter Phelan asked me to take her to a play that one of her best friends Josse had a role in. The show was named *White Christmas.* It was a play based on and totally true to the

Sundance and Cherokee Moon

movie dialogue from *White Christmas* with Bing Crosby, Danny Kaye, Rosemary Clooney (the internationally famous George Clooney's aunt) and Vera-Ellen. Josse was in the children's chorus. These young high school and younger students were so professional and had such excellent voices and acting ability that they could have been on Broadway. I sat there throughout the play filled with memories surrounding this movie in my life growing up and as an adult. I remembered so many lovely Christmases with my grandparents, my aunts and uncles, my cousins, my parents and my seven siblings, two brothers and five sisters, and with friends.

I remembered going to the train station with my mother, my maternal grandmother and grandfather Bess and Pat Phelan, my grandmother Katie Green, my aunts and uncles and my brother and sister waiting for the train to roll in at the Union Pacific Train Station in Omaha, Nebraska. A train was bringing my father home from the war in his Army uniform. I told Phelan that every Christmas since that movie has been on television, we always watch *White Christmas* at Christmas. This year was no exception.

Another annual film is *The Quiet Man* with John Wayne and Maureen O'Hara about the courting and marriage of an Irish woman and an Irish American man, a former boxer who refuses to fight. This film and other Irish films are always shown around St. Patrick's Day.

Sundance wasn't the first film festival I have attended. In 1980, my friend Mary Beth Fogarty (Mary Beth and her husband Ed Fogarty were close friends of mine) and me along with my twins Mary Kay and Elizabeth drove down the mountains of Colorado from Cripple Creek to the Telluride Film Festival Labor Day weekend. Like Park City, Telluride during the winter is a ski resort. In the summer it has its annual Labor Day Film Festival and annual Jazz Festival. After a few days of all of us visiting with friends Dave and Joanie Liddell in the house of my Omaha friend Barney McGuire in Criple Creek, Colorado, Mary Beth, my girls and I headed out for Telluride.

Leaving Cripple Creek, Colorado, we took the "Old Scenic Road" down to Telluride. Contrasted to the safety of transportation for the Sundance Festival, the trip down that old scenic road was treacherous. It wasn't a road; it was a narrow mountain path with all of us and the van clinging to the mountain side on our right to avoid death at the bottomless abyss on our left. Mary Beth got out at one pass and guided me around it. With a few wet pants and lots of anxiety we finely arrived safely at Telluride at night.

The beautiful September weather of Telluride just like the gentle snow and winter weather of Park City contributed to the pleasure of the festival. Both festivals featured workshops, as well as films, with stars, directors and screenwriters talking about each film and topic before and after the showing. At Telluride you had to go up a ski lift to get to the top where one workshop was held. Up there we sat on bales of hay to eat and listen. The sky was pure blue and the sun bright. While I was standing in line, a woman ahead of me was talking. "That's Jonathan Demme back there. He hasn't had a good movie since _____." I don't know if it was Johathan Demme, but Demme went on to be a major director and in 1992, he won the best director Academy Award for the picture 'Silence of the Lambs' and the picture also garnered best film, best screenplay, best actor and best actress awards. He has had many successes since then. As I said the sky was blue and the sun was shining. You only needed a light sweater. It was a beautiful and thrilling day.

The director each year at Telluride is a surprise. In 1980, the featured director was Werner Herzog, the great German director. His lead actor Klaus Kinsky was there as well and several of Herzog's films were featured. One morning at breakfast with my girls and Mary Beth, we spotted Klaus Kinsky at a nearby table eating breakfast with an attractive woman. Mary Beth and I told the girls who he was and encouraged them to get his autograph. Mary Kay was the brave one, and for her reward Klaus Kinsky gave her a kiss as well as an autograph.

Back at Sundance, the official program for the festival, with the theme of the year on the front cover, listed each movie, the producers, director, screenwriter, actors and actresses and a brief synopsis of each movie. I still have my festival program. The movies were listed in categories. There were the premiere movies including Louis Malle's *Au Revoir Les Enfants* and *Moonstruck* with Cher and Nicolas Cage and John Water's *Hair Spray.* There was dancing in the aisles at the end of *Hair Spray.*

Moonstruck was nominated for six Academy Awards or Oscars that year including Best Picture, Best Actress, Best Supporting Actor, Best Supporting Actress and Best Original Screenplay. Cher won for Best Actress, Olympia Dukakis won for Best Supporting Actress and John Patrick Shanley won for Best Original Screenplay.

Sundance and Cherokee Moon

Next there were the classic movies and also the feature films of director Samuel Fuller. My one year older brother Pat and I had seen many of Fuller's movies on our Sunday outings at the movies while we were kids. There were also the Argentine movies about the oppression during the years of the dictator Reynaldo Bignone where thousands of people were missing. The American film, *Missing* portrayed these atrocities where citizens disappeared and were murdered. And there were the first run independent films and documentaries up for competition shown at Sundance.

Every night starting at 8:00 p.m., a party was held for pass holders and people from the films and industry. Each party was put on by one of the sponsors of the festival. Each party had a theme, and the food at each party was unique and delicious. The night *Moonstruck* premiered, everyone from the movie was present at the party except Cher and Nicolas Cage who were absent from the festival. Actress Olympia Dukakis, the screenwriter John Patrick Shanley, the producer Patrick Palmer, and others from the movie were present. I got to visit with all of them about the movie. What great fun.

At the second party, Louise Levison, the film financier I met that first day, and I teamed up with famous writer Warren Adler, his wife Sonja, and his son. We would divide up the movies and report the next night whether they were "must see" or not.

Sonja and I had a mutual friend in Ceci Zorinsky, the wife of then Democrat, Nebraska U.S. Senator Ed Zorinksy. At the time of the festival Warren Adler was in negotiations for film rights to three of his many novels. He already had a movie deal for his book *The War of the Roses*, a black comedy about a divorcing couple. That movie came out in 1989 with Danny Devito directing himself, Michael Douglas and Kathleen Turner. One of those movies he had in negotiations at the festival was for his book *Random Hearts* which was made into a movie with Harrison Ford. Warren was on the phone regarding these movies and shared with us his conversations at night.

Dr. Ruth Westhiemer was at the festival, better known as televisions "Doctor Ruth" the famous sex therapist. She helped bring sex out of the dark ages with her compassionate answers. We visited together, and ended up in a theater together the next night. The movie was *Letters Home* about the Vietnam War. Hollywood stars read the actual letters of service men to their families sent before they died in battle and the film contained battle scenes with the audio voice over by famous actors reading the letters.

In 1970 to 1972, I was the military caseworker for U.S. Senator Harold E. Hughes from Iowa in his Washington, D.C. office. Senator Hughes was an anti-war Senator on the Armed Services Committee of the U.S. Senate and a Presidential candidate in 1971. Among my duties, I handled all the requests from service men and women for compassionate leave. I sat there in that dark theater sobbing as I watched the scenes of war shown as the letters were read. I particularly remember the letter from one young service man who needed leave to go home to marry his pregnant finance. I got the leave for him.

Actually all the letters were addressed to the Senator and went out with his signature. But as military caseworker, I would take the letters over to the office of the military liaison for all the branches of the military and make the requests. As a never married single mother, I felt special empathy for that young pregnant woman. Then the Senator got a letter from his mother telling the tragic news that he was on his way home to marry his fiancé when he stood up getting into a helicopter and the blade killed him. I was devastated. The war devastated us all, but that incident was particularly personal for me.

There was another Vietnam era movie that actually covered my job as a caseworker with the Senator. The 1979 movie is *Friendly Fire* with Carol Burnett and Sam Waterson about the Michael Mullin case. Michael Mullin was killed in Vietnam by our own troops, hence the title *Friendly Fire.* Senator Hughes worked for years to get the military to disclose the truth of Michael's death, and this was when Richard Nixon was President at the time. Three of us on the Senator's staff as military caseworkers worked on Michael Mullin's case: first Pat Dullery, then me and when I moved to Denver, Julie Holmes took over. Many years later back in Iowa, Julie Holmes married the then divorced Senator Hughes. The Senator and Julie are both deceased now.

In the movie, the Mullins did not give the Senator any credit for all the work he did. And years later we learned that Senator Hughes, who was an anti-war Senator on the Armed Services Committee, was on Nixon's "Enemies List." I got a letter addressed to the Senator from a constituent who said that Hughes' phones were tapped. I sent the letter under the

Sundance and Cherokee Moon

Senator's signature to the FBI. We got a cryptic answer: "There are no legal wiretaps on your phones." Obviously, there were illegal wiretaps. It came out in the Watergate hearings regarding the impeachment proceedings of President Richard Nixon.

Another movie that covered my work, this time as a clerk at the U.S. Department of Justice Civil Rights Division in 1965 and 1966, and was released later in 1988 was *Mississippi Burning.* The movie was about the murder of the three civil rights voter registration workers in Philadelphia, Mississippi. The three young men, Andrew Goodman, James Cheney and Michael Schwerner, were murdered by Klu Klux Klan law enforcement officers. Gene Hackman, William Defoe and Frances McDorman were the major actors in the film.

The Klansmen were all charged with murder in the state court and were acquitted by an all white jury. Next charges were filed in the U.S. District Court in Mississippi by the Civil Rights Division of the Department of Justice for a criminal conspiracy to violate the civil rights of the young workers. My former boss at Justice, Deputy Attorney General John Doar, tried that case. Seven men were all convicted. None of the men served more than six years in prison. That federal case was the United States v. Price. John Doar went on later to be chief counsel for the House Judiciary Committee for the impeachment of Richard Nixon and after that he had a successful law practice in New York.

My connection to the events that the movie portrayed was that as a docket room clerk I was assigned by my supervisor to review every document, photograph, and other piece of written evidence to assign them a docket number and send them on to the attorneys for each of the Southern districts to which they were assigned. We also got a lot of letters from victims of discrimination. One day, Mr. Doar came bursting into the docket room looking for photographs of Klansmen identified by one of their own who was an FBI informant. The envelope was directed to Mr. Doar, as was most of the mail coming into the Division. He said the man's life was in danger. I was able to tell him which attorney's desk the photographs were sent to. But after that it occurred to me that there was concern that there might be a Klan informant in the Division.

This Klan member FBI informant Gary Thomas Rowe was later tried and wrongfully acquitted along with three other Klan members for the murder of civil rights volunteer Viola Liusso, a white Unitarian Universalist and wife and mother from Detroit, Michigan. Rowe was one of four Klansmen in the car which forced Mrs. Liusso's car off the road and one of them shot and killed her near Selma, Alabama. The 19 year old young black civil rights volunteer with her played dead and was rescued. The White House or President Lyndon Johnson wanted to protect the identity of Rowe as an informant so his information could not be used in the trial.

I left the Civil Rights Division in 1966 in a state of profound depression or despair caused by all the evil I saw in those cases and in the other cases we could not handle. The pictures of the lynchings of black people for trying to register to vote still haunt me. Women's discrimination cases were boxed up and sent over to the Civil Rights Commission. The Southern Senators had inserted sex discrimination into the 1964 Civil Rights bill to try to defeat the Act. It didn't defeat the Act. That legislation triggered an avalanche of claims from women. The Division was only handling race discrimination complaints then, thus the women's complaints were sent over to the Civil Rights Commission. The EEOC, the Equal Employment Opportunity Commission was established by Congress to handle job discrimination complaints against private employers. The Justice Department Civil Rights Division handled employment discrimination complaints against state and local government agencies.

About 1970 while I was working for Senator Harold Hughes, John Doar came down from New York where he was working at the Bedford Stuyvesant Restoration Corporation, a Senator Robert F. Kennedy sponsored program, to give a speech to the Congressional Employees Association. (Robert F. Kennedy left the Justice Department as Attorney General to run for the U.S. Senate seat in New York.) I took Mr. Doar into the Senator's office to prepare his speech. He had some notes to go over. I attended the speech and met a few of the prominent civil rights lawyers who came to hear John Doar along with all of us Congressional employees.

Afterward I took Mr. Doar to the train station and waited with him for his train to New York. He asked me why I found it so frustrating to work for him. "It wasn't you," I told him. "It was all those people who were suffering injustice and discrimination, black people, women, gay people, older people and others committed to mental hospitals, so many more and there was no way to help them all." My major contribution to Mr. Doar was to advise him to establish a correspondence section to answer all the two day return Congressional requests and the letters from the public. When he placed me in the docket room, where I would wait to be an investigator, he asked me to find out how to straighten out the procedures there so the lawyers could get their mail and documents faster. I made several recommendations to him.

Eventually eleven years later, I would go to law school. My lawyer father inspired me and two of my brothers and two of my sisters and two of my cousins and four of our neighbors to become lawyers. I graduated in 1977. My father died in 1968 after the assassination of Robert F. Kennedy. Dad was the working Nebraska State co-chairman of the Senator's Presidential campaign just as he had been for President John F. Kennedy.

Dad suffered instant heart death after one of three reporters interviewing him at the Nebraska Democrat State Convention at Hastings, Nebraska, eight days after the assignation of Senator Robert Kennedy, asked him as chairman of the Kennedy delegation: "Where will the Kennedy delegates go now." With a pained expression on his face, he dropped dead. I never got to practice law with my father, something I always missed. Years later, a woman who spoke with my father the day he died told me that he was hoping I would go to law school and practice law with him. I asked her why she waited so many years to tell me.

My father inspired me to become a lawyer. Robert F. Kennedy and John Doar inspired me to become a civil rights lawyer. The late Benjamin Wall and the late Ernest Wintroub, my lawyer bosses when I was a law student, were the only plaintiffs' civil rights lawyers in the entire State of Nebraska for years. They trained me to be a civil rights lawyer. In 1963, I got to attend the Senate Judiciary hearing when Robert F. Kennedy introduced what would become the 1964 Civil Rights Act. I have spent most of my professional life enforcing that law.

This past year 2014 was the 50th anniversary of the passage of the 1964 Civil Rights Act and the need for the act is still great. The 1978 Pregnancy Discrimination Act, the Age Discrimination Act and the American Disability Act and the 1991 Civil Rights Act followed the passage of the 1964 Civil Rights Act. I enforced the 1964 Civil Rights Act starting as co-council in a successful major race discrimination employment discrimination law suit against the City of Omaha Fire Division as a senior law student in the U.S. District Court for Nebraska at Omaha. And I continued after graduation as a plaintiffs' employment discrimination attorney, with a few years out due to my bi-polar illness and I retired from private practice in January of 2015.

Sundance and Cherokee Moon

Even before all these movies that touched on my life was the movie *A Thousand Clowns* with Jason Robards and Barbara Harris. She played a child welfare worker and he played the uncle of a child welfare recipient threatened with losing custody of his young nephew. In one scene during a home visit, she tearfully tells the uncle about how she dreads seeing some clients and loves others. I laughed hysterically because as a county welfare case worker I understood her feelings, but I did love most of my clients and my clients loved me.

I was the only caseworker allowed to go into the black community after the 1967 riots in Omaha because of this mutual affection and respect for me in the community. It was after a home visit with a white woman and her beautiful young daughter where the mother told me the story of the sexual abuse she was subjected to as a child by her parents that I started praying for my clients. I went to the chapel of the Poor Clare Convent in Omaha and spent an hour of county time praying for that woman and all my clients.

I have continued that practice of praying for my clients for all my law clients as well. Ironically, I knew the man who fathered her beautiful daughter and I knew his attorney. It was my father. Because of confidentiality, I never discussed the case with my father. The settlement was only for $3,000.00 back in 1966.

This man was the only person with my beloved friend Author O'Leary as he died. It is all the stuff of a novel. The law is now that the parents of a child cannot enter into settlement about child support. It is the right of the child to receive support until they reach the age of majority. The mother can settle for loss of income and medical expenses, but she cannot settle for child support.

Many of the movies at the Sundance Film Festival in 1988 dealt with justice and civil rights issues both in the United States and in Central and South America. I grew up a World War II child and an American History major. But in the years working at the Justice Department and since, I learned that Hitler wasn't the only leader of genocide, and that evil wasn't limited to one race, one ethnic group, one sex or one nation. We have seen in the 20th and 21st centuries the story of Cain and Abel played out in oppression and genocide only to see it again and again—in Nigeria, in Rwanda, in the Sudan, in the Congo, in Central and South America and in

48

our own country during the 1950's and 1960's because of the Klu Klux Klan and other Southerners against black citizens who asserted their Constitutional right to vote, let alone the continuing millions of victims of domestic violence, violence and murder. And let me not forget the atrocities to which we subjected our Native Americans and slavery.

In the documentary competition there were two films of note on Central America. *Fire from the Mountain* is a history of the American war against Nicaragua. Another film is *The Houses Are Full of Smoke*, a movie portraying the atrocities in Guatemala, El Salvador and Nicaragua. This last film documents the attempts by our CIA to murder Father Miguel D'Escota, the Maryknoll priest serving as minister of defense in Nicaragua in the newly elected Sandinista government.

I met Father D' Escota in Omaha when I was on the Omaha City Council from 1977 to 1981. Our Democrat, U.S. Senator Ed Zorinsky invited several members of that new government to Omaha and sponsored a reception for them to meet local elected officials and members of the community. We invited them to come down to City Hall the next day for a tour. I was showing Father D' Escoto our new security cameras in our offices. He spoke: "I have those in my bedroom." I was stunned. I realized that his life was in constant danger and years later I learned that our CIA was behind the danger.

Pope John Paul II denied the priests like Father D'Escoto the right to say Mass and other priestly duties because of their "Liberation Theology" in helping to seek representation for the poor. For the last twenty-nine years Father has lived with his Maryknoll order. August 4th, 2014, Pope Francis restored all Father's and the others to their priestly duties. They can all say Mass again.

On March 24, 1980's in El Salvador, saintly Archbishop Oscar Romero was shot to death while he held the communion host up during Mass for adoration. It is my understanding that these men who murdered him were trained in the United States. I was on the Omaha City Council at the time and the news of his assassination was all over the nation. Catholics from the community and students at Creighton University when the word got out filed into St. John's Church on campus for a prayer vigil for him. Pope Francis has cleared the way for the beatification of Archbishop Romeo this year by declaring him a martyr. He will be the first liberation cleric beatified by the Catholic Church. He has finally been recognized as a martyr. Martyrs don't need miracles.

One of the acquaintances I made at the Sundance festival was the now late actor Cliff Robertson who was there as a representative of festival sponsor AT&T. He had also played with Robert Redford in *Three Days of the Condor,* one of my favorite films. Cliff Robertson played the corrupt CIA man who ordered all the murders. But the film I talked to him about was his role as Charlie in the movie *Charlie* about a mentally challenged man who was given new drugs that gave him above average intelligence. He had a romance with the woman doctor in charge of the experiment. In the movie *Charlie* the drugs tragically wore off and he returned to low I.Q. again.

When I went on Geodon, a new drug, in 2004 for my bi-polar illness, and it normalized my moods and enhanced my intellectual abilities by speeding up the timing of the synapses in my brain, I often worried if the effects would wear off like the drug did for Charlie, not that I was low IQ. There was an appreciable delay in processing new information on Lithium and I found no delay with Geodon. But eleven years later, that has not been my experience. Geodon continues to give me normal moods and faster synopses.

I wanted Cliff Robertson to know that in Omaha some psychiatrists, elected officials, parents and workers developed the Eastern Nebraska Community Office for the Retarded or ENCOR, a government agency that encompasses six counties. The program which promoted and provided normalcy and community based housing and treatment became a world-wide model and people from all other the world still come to ENCOR to be trained and to set up programs in their own countries.

Some of the same people involved in establishing ENCOR, along with the United States Department of Justice Civil Rights Division, filed a lawsuit against the governor and the state to end the warehousing of people with mental retardation at Beatrice State Home in Beatrice, Nebraska.

A settlement was reached with the State government and the Department of Justice and the Plaintiffs that the State would fund community based housing and treatment programs and return hundreds of people at Beatrice back to their communities through these programs. The settlement also entailed leaving some of the more severely handicapped individuals in Beatrice.

Today, some of those same people who supported the lawsuit along with others are still trying to close Beatrice. Their efforts increased after reports of the deaths of some of these severely handicapped people as a result of negligence and civil rights violations against the residents. Some staff members were prosecuted. But the facility still exists and the per diem patient costs of maintaining this facility far exceeds the cost of caring for these citizens in the community.

Cliff and I also talked about his film accounting lawsuit against the producer David Begelman. Robertson won the lawsuit, but the judge expunged the record after Begelman paid Robertson so that it wouldn't be a precedent. I told him about the outrageous conduct of Judge C. Arlen Beam in my race, sex and pregnancy discrimination case captioned Crystal Chambers v. The Omaha Girls Club et al. Judge Beam accepted the Girls Club's racially and sexually discriminatory reason for the firing of Crystal and the enactment of the single pregnancy negative role modeling policy.

The clubs' justification for enacting the single pregnant role modeling policy after firing Crystal was because of the number of illegitimate births in the black community. The first raised this defense before a secret hearing before the NEOC, the Nebraska Equal Opportunity Commission with no notice to Crystal Chambers. The judge ruled they could discriminate on the basis of race and sex because of that. He totally ignored the 1978 Pregnancy Discrimination Act and ruled that his decision was not a precedent. As a judge he knew that all cases are precedents if reported. (Now that all cases are handled online in the federal courts except for trial, the Judges don't save many of the cases so there are no precedents even for the good decisions.) We took the case all the way up to the Eighth Circuit Court of Appeals. The majority, with then newly appointed Appeals Court Judge C. Arlen Beam obstaining, denied our appeal for a hearing en banc or with the full court.

The Presiding Judge Donald P. Lay wrote a dissenting opinion joined by Judges Theodore McMilllian, one of a few black federal judges and the only black Eighth Circuit Judge, and Judge Gerald W. Heaney and found the discharge of Crystal Chambers and the enactment of the single pregnancy role modeling policy impermissible sex discrimination in violation of the 1978 Pregnancy Discrimination Act.

Sundance and Cherokee Moon

Years later in 2005 to 2007, I wrote a book about the case entitled *Women of Courage: The Rights of Single Mothers and Their Children Inspired by Crystal Chambers a New Rosa Parks* (Kindle, Amazon.com, Nook, Barnes&Noble.com, and I-Tunes.) See also www.marykaygreen.com, and on You Tube at "Women of Courage the Rights of Single Mothers," is my interview with Crystal Chambers Stewart. I'll show a bit of vanity and say that I have a better haircut now and I am thirty pounds lighter. Crystal is excellent. She went on after the case and married her daughter Ruthie's father Rodney Stewart and graduated from Bellevue University, in Bellevue, Nebraska, cum laude. Together, they raised Ruthie with fifteen foster teenagers, black, white and Native Americans.

I ordered the transcript of the Chambers trial from the clerk of U.S. District Court in Omaha so I could make copies. I had carried around for twenty years Crystal's copy of the transcript, but gave it up knowing that if I needed it I could make a copy from the court file. The file and the fifteen volume transcript had mysteriously disappeared. Had it been accidentally or deliberately misfiled in the underground storage facility in Kansas City? I will never know. All I can tell you is that lawyers and citizens cannot check out federal files. The files do not leave the court house unless they are sent to storage. You can photo copy them in the clerk's office but you can't take them out, or the clerk can send them to a safe copy center to be copied for you to later pick the copies up at the federal clerk's office. Only judges and their law clerks and secretaries can check the files out. Suspicious, isn't it.

At Sundance, I was still waiting for my opportunity to meet Robert Redford. My effort was a little like finding "Waldo" in the Children's book of that name. He never came to any other evening party that I attended except the first one when he was stuck in the stairwell. Once in the theater in my motel in came Robert Redford right before the lights went down and he sat right in front of me. Alas, he was sitting next to a famous movie critic and they left as soon as the title screen came on. Another time, he sat three rows behind me.

While I didn't get to meet Robert Redford during the festival, I met him vicariously. I became friends with a Hispanic film group, a writer, producer, director and actors in a movie titled *Break of Dawn.* The movie told the story of Pedro Gonzales, an Hispanic man from Mexico who came to the Los Angeles area in the 1930's and became a famous morning radio

52

talk show host and a political activist. Gonzales who was a singer and guitarist became increasingly vocal about the oppression of Mexican and Hispanic peoples in California. As a result he was the victim of a plot to falsely accuse him of rape of a minor. He was convicted by perjured testimony and served in San Quentin until his wife and thousands of Hispanic people were able to organize a campaign for his parole. At the time of the festival he was working on full exoneration and a pardon and had returned to live in California after years back in Mexico.

On January 22, 1988, my new friends, the writer-director Isaac Artenstein, the producer and the actors were invited by Robert Redford to screen their movie down at Sundance where their audience was Robert Redford and Nobel laureate Gabriel Garcia Marquez author of *One Hundred Years of Solitude,* (who died April 17, 2014 at age 87: he received the Noble Prize in Literature in 1982 for all his books). Also down at Sundance for the viewing was the actor Ruben Blasé from Robert Redford's new film *The Milagro Beanfield Wars,* a movie about a man who talked to the saints. I loved that movie when I got to see it. Isaac Artenstein, the director and writer of the screen play of *Break of Dawn* reported that his film was well received by his famous audience.

In the screenwriting course I was taking that January at the University of Nebraska at Omaha during the time I attended the festival, my final submission, not a screenplay, was my report on the festival which I titled: "Heart and Conscience: A Report on the United States Film Festival Sponsored by the Sundance Institute." My professor James Devney, a Hollywood screenwriter himself, liked my report and later attended one of the screenwriters' workshops at Sundance. After the class was over, I wrote a screenplay titled *They Let Mothers in Law School?* It is about my three years in Creighton University Law School in the first large class of women, there were thirty of us, and the first class of mother, there about ten of us. I asked professor Devney to read it and he pronounced it good. I am publishing my screenplay on Amazon this year too.

I never got to meet Robert Redford at the festival, but I did get to greet him in Omaha in 1996. Robert Redford's son Jamie Redford came to Omaha to have a liver transplant at the University of Nebraska Medical Center Liver Transplant Center in 1995. Robert Redford lived in Omaha during his son's surgery and recovery. On October 28, 1996, Robert Redford, Jamie Redford and Peter Buffett, a musician, and friend of Jamie Redford and son of Omaha financier Warren Buffett, held a fundraiser to provide money for Jamie to make a film to promote organ donation. Robert Redford spoke as did Jamie Redford and Peter Buffett played the piano in a performance with Native Americans.

The fundraiser was to benefit the James Redford Institute for Transplant Awareness, and it was held at the Rose Blumkin Performing Arts Center, (the former Astro Movie Theater I had a role in preserving as a City Council member who helped block its destruction which became known as "The Rose," after Rose Blumkin who bought and renovated the theater. (Rose Blumkin was the founder of the Nebraska Furniture Mart in Omaha. She was known as mean to her employees. Warren Buffet, the famous Omaha financier, bought her 80% share of the company for his Berkshire Hathaway Holding Company). That tradition was carried out by some of her relatives.

At the break during the performance, it was announced that Robert Redford wanted to greet everyone who attended, and that we should form a single line so Mr. Redford could come and greet everyone, one at a time. I was standing next to a wonderful woman named Liz Karnes who I knew as an activist for quality education. She was struggling with cancer. She later died of the disease. Liz and I exchanged words about our mutual excitement of getting to meet Robert Redford. When it was my turn to shake hands with him and to hear his "Thank you for coming, and supporting my son's film," I melted into those eyes and said: "Thank you, Mr. Redford." At last, I got to meet Robert Redford.

November 6, 1996, I wrote a fan letter to Robert Redford talking about my trip to his film festival, learning that he had a panic attack the opening night, deciding to pray for him and my favorite actors and people in the entertainment industry as a result, living in Overland Park, Kansas at the time where you have to get there a half hour early to get a seat at the movies, spending that time to pray for my "friends" in the entertainment industry, learning that his son had a transplant at the University of Nebraska Medical Center where I went for medical care for the then past twenty years, and that the people of Omaha were graciously greeting him and his son, talking about how so many of his films portrayed incidents in my own life starting with *The Way We Were* and *Up Close and Personal* and *All the President's Men.*

I talked about how my eight year old grandson Michael loved him as much as I did. Years later my mother refused to go to the emergency room until

Sundance and Cherokee Moon

Redford's movie 'The Horse Whisperer' ended. She was having shooting pains down her left arm. She apparently had a transient incident, but nothing showed up on the tests. It passed and she was well.

I sent Robert Redford a picture of my grandson and his friend, a picture of Redford himself that the nurse Delores Siglin sitting next to me at the program took of him (she gave me copies and permission to use her photograph) and a picture I took of my late father James F. Green, Robert F. Kennedy's Nebraska State Presidential campaign chairman, standing by Robert Kennedy who was sitting watching the election returns for his victory in the Nebraska May 1968 primary.

I also loved *Three Days of the Condor* and *Butch Cassidy and the Sundance Kid* as well as all *The Sting* movies. *All The President's Men* is one of my all-time favorite movies. My favorite movie is *To Kill A Mockingbird.* Gregory Peck played the attorney Atticus Finch who defended a black man falsely accused of raping a white woman in the South. My father was Atticus Finch. Like the character Atticus Finch, my father inspired many to become lawyers. My grandchildren loved this movie and watched it with me over and over. My third favorite movie is *Casa Blanca* with Humphrey Bogart and Ingrid Bergman. I am an incurable romantic.

Robert Redford won his directorial Oscar for the movie *Ordinary People* about the Jarret family and the impact the accidental drowning death of the oldest son has on the family. The mother becomes cold and bitter toward the son who survived and that son becomes guilt ridden and severely depressed and suicidal. The son gets help from a compassionate psychiatrist and eventually the father leaves the wife and establishes a home for the son and himself. This is Robert Redford's mental health movie. I loved all of Robert Redford's movies starting with *Butch Cassidy and the Sundance Kid* with Paul Newman. His only movie that I didn't like was *An Indecent Proposal.* I hated his character.

Robert Redford wrote back. I was thrilled. He wrote: "Thank you for your kind words and thoughts. Your letter is my reward. Robert Redford." I still have that letter. Two years ago, my daughter Elizabeth gave me a copy of the book *Robert Redford: The Biography* by Michael Feeney Callan. I learned to appreciate him even more for his work for the environment and in politics. There were more details of his activism in the book than I had realized. He is a wonderful human being. I'd love to have lunch with him someday. I do get emails and mail from him promoting progressive and environmental causes, like many people do, on that same stationery.

This year, 2014, Robert Redford had a major role in the popular franchise *Captain America.* The movie is a blockbuster internationally. He played the villain. May you have a long, active life, Robert Redford. I will always be in your audience as long as I can breath and have all my faculties.

Speaking of being a movie fan, it turns out Pope Francis is one too. He recently listed two movies as his favorite movies of all time. These two movies are the 1954 movie *La Strada,* an Italian movie by Federico Fellini, the great Italian screenwriter and director, staring Anthony Quinn and Guilietta Masina, and *Open City,* a 1945 movie about the underground resistance fighters in Italy against the German occupation during World War II in Rome.

I hope the Pope got to see the movie 'Philomena" and that the Vatican kept its word about releasing the birth and adoption records of the children taken from the unwed mothers in Ireland called the Madgalenes.

CHAPTER 2: LAW CASES 1988.

My attorney friends Ed Diedrich and Ed Fogarty and I had appealed Crystal Chambers case against the Omaha Girls Club et al to the full Eighth Circuit Court of Appeals. February 25, 1988, we got the denial of the majority of the judges to give us a new hearing en banc, or before the full court. Included in the opinion was the strong dissenting opinion of Chief Judge Donald P. Lay joined by Judges Gerald W. Heaney and Theodore McMillian. They found the Girls Club's single pregnancy negative role modeling policy and its discharge of our client Crystal Chambers, a twenty-one year old single, black, pregnant, arts and crafts instructor, impermissible sex segregation and a violation of the 1978 Pregnancy Discrimination Act.

Judge C. Arlen Beam, the trial judge, ignored the overwhelming evidence in support of Crystal's case and totally ignored and made no mention or ruling on the 1978 Pregnancy Discrimination Act. He ruled that the Girls Club could racially discriminate "because of the high rate of illegitimate births in the black community." At the three judge panel hearing before our appeal to the full 8th Circuit, two of the judges upheld the lower court decision by Judge C. Arlen Beam still ignoring the 1978 Pregnancy Discrimination Act. The third judge on that panel, Judge Theodore McMillian, dissented and cited the 1978 Pregnancy Discrimination Act. Judge McMillian was the only black judge on the Eighth Circuit Court of Appeals and one of the few black federal judges. He ruled on the 1978 Pregnancy Discrimination Act and found the club had violated it.

In a speech before the Federal Bar Association, Chief Judge Donald P. Lay cited his dissenting opinion in Crystal Chambers v. the Omaha Girls Club as one of the twelve most important decisions he wrote on the bench as a federal judge. (It was Judge Olay who encouraged me to write a book about the case when I sent him a short summary about it.) And Judge Theodore McMillian was honored by the Kansas City Bar Association for his dissenting opinion at the three judge panel hearing Crystal's case. Google or search: "Crystal Chambers v. Omaha Girls Club" for all three of the court decisions, especially Chief Judge Lay's dissenting opinion, joined by Judges Gerald W. Heaney and Theodore McMillian. The case was the topic of over one hundred law review articles with most of the early decisions siding with Crystal. It is also taught in the Employment Law casebook in every law school in America.

When I sent a letter along with a copy of Judge Beam's decision to the U.S Senate Judiciary Committee to oppose his nomination to the Eighth Circuit Court, I was contacted by an attorney with the committee and informed that I was the only Nebraska attorney to oppose his nomination. I was asked to poll the other civil rights attorneys. I did and I reported back that they all wanted him out of the district court, the trial court, because most employers don't appeal decisions when the Plaintiffs win in trial.

Judge Beam was grilled during his Judiciary Committee hearing about his decision, but his nomination was sent to the full Senate where he was confirmed. I was promised by my contact on the committee staff that at the next amendments to the 1964 Civil Rights Act there would be a provision barring the business necessity defense, the Girls Club's defense, in cases where intentional discrimination is alleged. That provision is part of the 1991 Civil Rights Act, section 105 (a) (2). When I informed the Girls Club of the provision in the new law and one of their patrons, Omaha based financier Warren Buffett, the Girls Club eliminated their single pregnancy negative role modeling policy. They no longer discriminate against single pregnant employees, black or white. The Omaha Girls Club is an excellent club now. Warren's daughter Susie Buffett is a sponsor of the club as well and active with the national Girls Club and Warren is a patron of the Club.

In 1986 before, during and after the trial in Crystal's case, we were interviewed by the national media. We were on NPR, National Public Radio's "All Things Considered" in a twenty minute piece by reporter Jackie Lyden and a ten minute follow up when Judge Beam's decision came down; the case was reported in *Newsweek*, the *New York Times*, *The New York Daily News*, *In These Times* and other papers. Crystal and I and Ed Diedrich and his client Jeanne Eckmann (her case was made into a movie *Cast the First Stone*), Sheri Long from Omaha and her client Pamela Simmons a former staff member at the Girls' Club and other single mother teachers were on the Phil Donahue *Donahue* daily talk show in New York City, New York.

I still have copies of the *Donahue* show and the clippings from newspapers and *Newsweek*. Apparently the staff on Donahue's show did not save the tape, so I may have three of the only copies.

Sundance and Cherokee Moon

Next, I represented a young, white wife who worked for the same company as her husband. An older male worker had been sexually harassing her and at one point brought into work a twelve inch screw, showed it to her and gestured that he had the equipment to do it to her. We went all the way to the state president of the company and met with him, the husband and wife and me, and I told the president about the sexual harassment by the older, white male employee. The couple was white. The president's refusal to take the twelve inch duplicate screw when I offered it to him showed he understood the offensiveness of the original screw. The president offered the husband an agency if he and his wife dropped the sexual harassment charge. They did and he kept his word.

Following that, I was hired again by Judy Danielson, the brilliant psychologist at the Women's Prison at York, Nebraska, called "York." I represented her years earlier when the new male warden started an intimate relationship with her shortly after his arrival at the prison, and then he dumped her for another woman employee. He used the female prison staff for sexual purposes, a violation of the 1964 Civil Rights Act. What he also did wrong was to fire my client when he was done with her. I contacted the Director of the Nebraska prisons and met with him with my client. Five days later she was reinstated to her job and the male warden was out of a job and out of the state. It didn't hurt that the Governor was a woman named Kay Orr, a fairly good governor.

Judy Danielson was the psychologist who worked for years to help Caril Ann Fugate rehabilitate so that she was eventually paroled after seventeen years in prison. Caril Ann had been the fourteen year old companion of nineteen year old Charles Starkweather who went on a killing spree through Nebraska and Wyoming December, 1957 and January, 1958 killing eleven people. Starkweather was executed June 25, 1958. Judy Danielson's work with Caril Ann Fugate and other women inmates was brilliant.

There were movies made about this rampage: *The Sadist* (1963), *Badlands* (1973), *Kalifornia* (1993), *Natural Born Killer* (1994) and *Starkweather* (2004). The plot of many segments of television series was based on the Starkweather-Fugate relationship and a number of books were written about this case. The famous American author Stephen King was said to be deeply affected by the Starkweather-Fugate murder spree and is said to have based some of his characters on that pairing.

59

Judy Danielson was fired again. This time she was fired by the Warden who as deputy warden replaced the fired Warden. That Warden was the deputy Warden in the original case. He retaliated against Danielson, but the Federal Judge ruled years later that an eight year span between the original discrimination and the retaliatory discharge was too great.

When Judy and I went to York to take the deposition of the Warden, his secretary, a blond, buxom, fully breasted woman, who wore a tight, pink, sweater dress that clung to her body and the hem landed half way up between her knees and her hips. Judy told me that she had reported to the Warden that the inmates and the staff felt that he and his secretary had an "inappropriate relationship." This was before he fired Judy.

No doubt the Warden had informed his secretary of his conversation with Judy. She knew that we would be there on this date to depose him and she defiantly dressed provocatively. If the Warden wasn't having an inappropriate relationship with this overtly sexual woman than he must have been a eunuch.

At any rate the 300 days from the date Judy confronted the Warden for the filing of new federal charges of sexual harassment and retaliation charges for addressing it had passed.

Now the federal judges in the conservative 8th Circuit are saying that the retaliation is not actionable if there is two months or more between the discrimination and the retaliation. Clearly, the courts are trying to reduce the number of discrimination and retaliation cases filed in federal court. There is no legal justification for these decisions. It is a clear example of conservative federal judges judicially legislating to change federal civil rights laws and to void the famous retaliation discrimination 2006 U.S. Supreme Court decision titled Burlington Northern and Sante Fe Railway v. White.

I had a case in 2014 where the federal judge applied the two month rule to continuing discrimination and further it was a she said and she said case and he ruled in favor of the manager who openly lied about everything against the employee, a very honest and truthful young woman I have known from the day of her birth (the jury would have loved her) when the credibility or believability of the parties and witnesses is clearly an issue to be determined by the jury. It was a wrong decision.

Sundance and Cherokee Moon

Nearly all of my cases since 1988 have settled after filing charges with the EEOC or after filing a case in federal court. I have not had a civil rights trial since then. My retirement from private practice was January of 2015, in a case concerning the discrimination of two black older female public employees. It was resolved against a government entity two years after the original and continuing discrimination began. Judy Danielson's original case, as I earlier noted, was settled five days after I contacted the Director of Corrections and before any EEOC charge was filed. This was an exception as was the case of sexual harassment after the meeting the company president.

That August in 1988, I represented six employees of the Omaha Employees Betterment Association known as the EBA, a civil rights organization, suing the City of Omaha and the civilian union. The trial had been in its second week when the lead attorney for the City had a mild heart attack. The judge denied my opposition to the City's Motion for a one month recess in the trial and gave the City the one month delay. He did this after telling us that when he was a young associate in his law firm, the lead trial attorney had a heart attack and the judge in that case made him continue to try the case, and that he had won the case.

Yet in our case, he didn't make the female deputy city attorney continue with the case. I took the judge's decision in the EBA case as one of adversely assessing the competence of the woman deputy city attorney. (By the way, that woman attorney was the law clerk for Judge Beam in Crystal's lawsuit because all the rest of his law clerks had conflicts of interest. She did also since she had written the sex education program for the Girls Club but we didn't think she would ignore the law or would she just be writing what the judge ordered her to, i.e., to ignore the extensive briefing by Ed Fogarty on the 1978 Pregnancy Discrimination Law. I had done extensive research on the Pregnancy Discrimination law before filing Crystal Chamber's original charges of discrimination, but Ed did a great job of writing that portion of our brief from my research).

When the jury came back from the one month recess in the E.B.A. case, the trial took another four weeks including the City's defense and the Union's defense. The jury came in with a verdict for only one of the plaintiffs, a woman named Avis Linstrom, and she got the job she applied for as a 911 Operator. When I polled the jury, they said they had forgotten the earlier evidence because of the one month recess, but one woman had identified with Avis and she convinced the jury to find in her favor. The only other case I was familiar with where the judge gave a one month recess in a trial was in the criminal case of New York crime lord John Gotti. Gotti was acquitted. The Gotti trials are called the Pizza Trials. A book was written with that title. I read it.

Rather than giving me and my partner on the case Elizabeth Kountze credit for the work we had done on the case, the judge accepting the argument of the now recovered Deputy City Attorney divided our attorney fee application and only awarded us 1/6th of our fee request or $15,000.00 for a major civil rights victory that took two years of preparation and discovery. He later told his law clerk that he had not done justice in our case. The law clerk told another attorney who told me. I don't know if the judge elaborated about his award of the one month recess for the Deputy City Attorney or his outrageous attorney fee award or both. Ironically it was the same judge who had awarded Alan Kirchen and me that big attorney fee award in Rudy Avila's case.

I believed the Judge was punishing us on the attorney fee award because Elizabeth and I brought out the fact that the now deceased lead male Deputy City Attorney's drinking during the trial made it more difficult. The judge ordered our affidavit sealed and chastised us for telling the truth. Also ironically the Deputy City Attorney was arrested for DUI (driving under the influence of alcohol) right after the trial. The city paid the paltry $15,000.00 attorney fee award for Betty Kountze and me for a major civil rights victory for Avis Linstrom worth thousands of dollars in attorney fees. I used part of my share to pay for my mother and me to go to Medjugorje in October that year of 1988.

Before that trial, Father Bill Whelan gave me a message from the Lord on this case when I asked him to pray for my clients. He told me up at the Communion rail after Mass after silent prayer that all the people involved in the case would turn against me. I was stunned. At the end of the trial the clients and the judge turned against me over the issue of attorney fees. The clients and I reconciled. Betty and I were upset by the Judge's decision, but we liked him personally. I still do. Good judges sometimes make bad decisions.

He later showed courage and bucked the mandatory federal sentencing act by ignoring the unequal recommended sentences for crack cocaine and powder cocaine possession which mandated stiffer sentences for crack cocaine. Whites used powder cocaine and got lighter sentences while blacks used crack cocaine and got twice the years in jail that white users got. Because of the judge's courage in opposing this injustice and the courage of other federal judges, the law was changed.

CHAPTER 3: MEDJUGORJE 1988

I did not hear about the Blessed Mother of Jesus' apparitions in Medjugorje until the winter of 1987. My lifetime friend Helen Abdouch, (who my family met and became close to when we were all working on President Kennedy's Presidential campaign in Omaha), talked to me one day about the Blessed Mother's apparitions in Medjugorje and the fact that an Omaha religious group called the Intercessors of the Lamb was holding monthly Masses with talks afterward about Medjugorje at St. Margaret Mary's Church. The group also took groups of people called pilgrims to Medjugorje.

The two greatest apparition sites recognized by the Catholic Church are Fatima in Portugal where the Blessed Mother appeared to the three young children ten and under and Lourdes in France where the Blessed Mother appeared to young teen Bernadette. But the apparitions in Medjugorje have been ongoing since June 24, 1981, and they continue to date.

On June 25, 2014, after the 33rd anniversary of her apparitions, the Blessed Mother told the visionaries that she would continue to appear by the grace of God. Some people had speculated that the apparitions would end at the 33rd year because that was the age of Jesus when he died on the cross. These apparitions are the longest apparitions in the history of mankind. And in each apparition, the Blessed Mother gives messages for all people to the six young visionaries to whom she appears who are now in their mid to late forties.

In 1987, I spoke to my mother at St. Margaret Mary's Church in Omaha about all this and asked her if she wanted to go to a Medjugorje Mass at St. Margaret Mary's. She said: "Yes." We went to the next monthly Mass. After Mass, Sr. Mary Nadine, the foundress of the group, introduced a priest who had been to Medjugorje with the Intercessors. He emphasized that the apparitions had been ongoing for six years. He told the story about the six young people, Vicka, Ivanka, Mirjana, Marije, Ivan and Jacob, and the early years of the apparitions of the Blessed Mother to them.

He read the monthly message the Blessed Mother gives to the world on the 25th of each month. (At that time you could hear the messages by calling a phone number but now you can access them at www.medjugorje.com, www.mejugorje.org or www.mej.com. Then the priest told how the Communist government persecuted the young visionaries, as they are called, forcing them to take all kinds of psychological and neurological tests to try to prove that their visions were fraudulent. The youngsters passed all the tests. Some few years later, the government decided it could profit from the millions of pilgrims who came to Medjugorje so they subsidized private homes and hostels with the host families paying a portion of the rents paid by pilgrims to the government. Since then, there have been over forty million pilgrims to Medjugorje and the people just keep coming and coming, people of all nationalities, races and countries including the United States.

Our Lady's purpose for the apparitions is to bring everyone to her Son, Our Lord Jesus Christ, and to bring peace to the world through the prayers of all peoples. She is called Our Lady Queen of Peace of Medjugorje— "peace in our hearts, peace in our homes, and peace in the world."

The Message for November 25, 1987, was:

"Dear children, today I call each one of you to decide to surrender again everything completely to me. Only that way will I be able to present each of you to God. Dear children, you know that I love you immeasurable and that I desire each of you for myself, but God has given to all a freedom which I lovingly respect and humbly submit to. I desire, dear children, that you help so that everything that God has planned for this parish shall be realized. If you do not pray, you shall not be able to recognize my love and the plan of God for this parish, and for each individual. Pray that Satan does not entice you with his pride and deceptive strength. I am with you and I want you to believe me that I love you. Thank you for having responded to my call."
(The Medjugorje Messages, Steve Shawl, the Medjugorje Web, 772 N. Peace Road, DeKalb, IL 60115, http://www.medjugorje.org).

Father described the miracles Our Lady rewards pilgrims with for coming to honor her and to pray with her. A major miracle is the Miracle of the Sun. People can look at the sun and see it as a gold circle, or a bright yellow circle with a large round white shape like a white communion host covering it. Sometimes the area around the sun is pink, purple, lavender, orange or gold with these various colors radiating around the sun with the sun pulsating in the sky. It is dangerous to look directly into the sun so it is not recommended unless you are in Medjugorje.

A smaller miracle is having the silver chains on your rosary turn to gold. People have had these gold chains tested, and they have proven to be real gold. (The rosary is a set of prayers using five sets of ten beads each to keep track of the prayers. The prayers are the Apostles Creed, the Our Father, the Hail Mary, and the Glory Be to the Father. There are four sets of the mysteries of the rosary, the Joyful, the Sorrowful, the Glorious and the Luminous. The beads are often held together by silver chains. It is these silver chains that turn to gold). Next to the Mass, the rosary is considered one of the most powerful prayers by the Catholic Church and Catholics.

My mother and I went to Medjugorje in October, 1988 with our chaplain Father Thomas Halley, S.J., a Jesuit priest of the Charismatic Renewal. Pope Francis is a Jesuit. Father Halley told us that the rosary would be said twice before the American Mass at 10:00 a.m. and twice before the International Mass at 4:30 p.m. right before the Blessed Mother's apparition to Ivan in the choir loft, and he encouraged us to pray the rosary at other times during each day and evening.

Father told how the rosary is said by pilgrims and others while climbing Apparition Hill where the Blessed Mother first appeared to the young visionaries, and climbing Mt. Krizevak where she also appeared. Mt. Krizevak is also known as Cross Mountain because in 1933, the villagers carried all the materials up the mountain to build a huge several ton stone cross. Our Lady told the visionaries that the inspiration years ago to the villagers was part of her plan for Medjugorje, and she also told them that the inspiration to the villagers to rebuild St. James Church after a fire to a much larger church was also part of her plan.

At one of the Medjugorje Masses in Omaha, a documentary film was shown of the village, St. James Church, Apparition Hill and Mt. Krizevak or Cross Mountain and the grape arbors between the church and the visionaries' homes. The film showed the Miracle of the Sun, a huge gold-orange sun with gold-orange pulsating around it. The film inspired deep feelings of reverence, and in the case of my mother and me a desire to go, but now was not possible.

Sundance and Cherokee Moon

My mother and I and our friend Helen attended all the monthly Medjugorje Masses at St. Margaret Mary's Church. There is a legend that Our Lady calls you if you are to go to Medjugorje and that she provides the money for you to go. The three of us did not feel the call until the next fall. Time and money were the two main issues in our going there. Time and money were especially issues for me. I had a busy year ahead of me in 1988.

After a Medjugorje Mass in August, 1988, Helen motioned us over to the pew where she was sitting. She had her purse open and she told my mother and me that God told her to give us money. She handed me a fist full of dollars and some change. The next month, she told us that God wanted her to give us the money to go to Medjugorje. This was a definite sign that my mother and I should go to Medjugorje, but I told Helen we could only accept her money if it was a loan. We signed up in September for an early October pilgrimage. Ten days before we were scheduled to go, I got my share of the legal fee Betty Kountze and I got from the city. I immediately deposited the check, paid Betty and made out a check to Helen and took it to her house to reimburse her for our trip.

My mother and I learned that Father Thomas Halley, S.J. would be our spiritual director for the trip and that there would be thirty-six of us. I had first met Father Halley, the summer before my sophomore year in high school. A young man I had become friends with came over to our house to get me. He had to wait because we were having a family portrait taken with my parents and my seven siblings and me.

(I remember the special light blue dress I wore that day. I so loved that dress and that day so much that I still have the dress saved in my trunk, the trunk I was required to buy when I entered the Sisters of Mercy in Omaha as a postulant in 1960 in September. I left in May of 61. I have kept all my favorite things and mementos in that trunk including the dress I wore to the White House where I got to visit with President Kennedy. It is stainless).

While I was in the convent in early November of 1960, my beloved grandmother Bess Phelan was hospitalized. The convent sent me with another sister, an older sister, to see her in the hospital. Seeing her so sick was hard on me. My grandmother and I were soul mates. After my grandfather Pat Phelan died, I spent a lot of time with my grandmother. One day I was up in the attic going through the trunk of formals belonging to my mother and her three sisters that they wore in college. I came down stairs and entered the dining room where my grandmother was sitting in

67

her red leather chair where she said her prayers every day and I noticed that she had a radiant smile on her face. I asked her why she was so happy. She told me that she heard footsteps coming up the stairs from the basement. When she looked at the door between the dining room where she was seated and the kitchen, she saw my grandfather. He smiled at her and said: "How're you doing Bessie?" And then he was gone.

Close to Thanksgiving 1960, I had an overwhelming premonition that my grandmother was dying. I went to our postulant mistress and begged her to let me go see my grandmother because she was dying. She said: "No, you are being selfish since you saw her earlier in the month." Two days later our postulant mistress came to see me. She apologized to me and told me that my grandmother had just died. It broke my heart not being able to say goodbye to her.

I suffered deep grief and depression over the death of my grandmother. I couldn't eat. I lost fifty pounds over the next few months. I told my postulant mistress that I wanted to go home and that I didn't want to be a nun anymore. I had had psychic experiences before and I felt that I would be frustrated in the convent if they were always denied like my premonition about my grandmother's death. Further I decided I wanted to get married and have children of my own. I left in May after I was interviewed by Dr. James Mahoney, M.D., the head of Psychiatry at Creighton Medical School who was giving mental health lectures to all the sisters.

A lot of pressure was put on me to stay in the convent. My postulant mistress told me that if I stayed, I would be mother general one day. This was not my ambition. She told me that if I left, I would never be able to accept a man's love since I was turning my back on Christ as my spouse. Worse than that was the pressure put on me by the novice mistress.

Every month when I said I wanted to leave, I was sent to the novice mistress and every month she told me horror stories about what happened to other girls who left and "turned their back on God." She said that God punished them and their families. The last story she told me before I left was about one of the older girls from Mercy High School who left and got married and had two children. They all died in a head on car crash coming back from Lincoln, Nebraska. God had punished that girl, she told me.

Sundance and Cherokee Moon

Well Dr. Mahoney told me that it was my life and I was the one who got to decide what I did with it. He told me if you decide to leave, come see me and I will help you readjust from convent life (I saw him off and on for a couple of years and he wanted me to go to medical school and to become a psychiatrist like him while my dad wanted me to become a lawyer and practice with him. My dad won out after his death). Next, I was called in to the main office. The Mother General of the Sisters of Mercy was visiting in Omaha. I was told to see her. She was very gentle and compassionate. Like Dr. Mahoney, she told me that it was my decision alone as to whether I would stay in the convent or leave and go back home. I told her that I wanted to leave. She said: "You go with my blessing, child." I called my parents and they came and picked me up. The rest is history.

Back in 1957, my friend took me out to Creighton Prep, the Jesuit High School for boys where he and his older brother and my older brother, who were friends and debate partners, were students. He wouldn't tell me who we were to meet, just a special person. When we got there, he took me up and introduced me to Father Thomas Halley, S.J., his favorite teacher, his English teacher. I have never forgotten that day and that meeting. The young man and Father Halley would become very important in my life.

The young man Jim Gleason years later would become my twin daughters' father in 1969, his behavior was not always good after that, and Father Halley, who was our chaplain in 1988 on our pilgrimage to Medjugorje who became my close friend and one of my spiritual advisors. My mother and Helen and I would be close to Father Halley attending his weekly Legion of Mary prayer group until his death years later from Parkinson's disease and pneumonia. He would save one of his two Masses he got to say each day for that weekly evening meeting and he would say Mass for our group in St. John's Church on the Creighton campus after the meeting. It was a special evening once a week.

Father Halley was a Charismatic priest like Father Whelan and like Father Whelan he had the gift of healing. Father Halley also had the gift of bi-location like many of the saints. In 1995, Helen had a near fatal asthma attack. She was able to call 911, and someone in her voice (she says it could not have been her because she was unconscious when the paramedics came) told me she was being taken to Creighton St. Joseph Hospital. I called Father Halley and he immediately left to meet her at the hospital.

Helen later told me that Father Halley was there at her bed in the Emergency Room just after she had been put on oxygen, an IV and all the monitors. A bed had been secured for her in the intensive care unit because she was so ill. She was being prepared to be taken there. Father Halley took her hand and prayed over her. Almost immediately the nurses came in and unhooked her from everything and told her she was being released. At this moment her brother Vral Popa and his wife entered the room. Father Halley walked over to them and told them that she was at the gates of Heaven but the Lord sent her back, then he left.

I lost a very close friend in Washington, D.C. named Iyla Gillispie who died at age forty from an asthma attack, and I had a close relative in a coma for five days after an asthma attack. And my friend here Melba Meyers' husband Charles died of an asthma attack after his doctor refused to refile his enhaler without an appointment. Asthma is a very serious illness.

In September, 1988, three weeks before we left for Medjugorje, I got an inner speaking or inner locution. The words that I heard interiorly were: "I have work for you to do and all I ask is that you be celibate unless you marry." I had an immediate knowing that it was God talking to me. I was thrilled but not surprised because in 1982, when I thought I was dying, I gave God the rest of my life to do whatever He wanted to do with it. A few years later, I took a vow of celibacy. I had not been without romance in my life and I thought it might be difficult, but I must have been given a special grace because it has never been a burden.

I have never been a wealthy person, so I couldn't give all my money to the poor like St. Elizabeth of Hungary or St. Francis of Assisi, but I did have that one gift, the gift of my life to give to God. At the time, I didn't think this commitment would be a long commitment. I was having serious health problems and I was convinced that I didn't have long to live. But here I am writing this book at age 73. Every day that I wake up is a pleasant surprise.

In the late 1980's God surrounded me with other people that He talked to beside Father Halley and Father Bill Whelan. Father Whelan is now Monsignor William S. Whelan and he has written a book about God's blessings on him. The book is titled *An Ordinary Priest Gifted By God's Grace.* Father Whelan is the healing priest whose weekly healing Masses my mother and I had been attending with Helen and others since 1982. In his book, which was written mainly for seminarians, Father Bill Whelan documents the fact that Jesus started talking to him at his first parish St. Michaels in South Sioux City, Nebraska. He documents when he received the gift of healing too. The book can be obtained from Standard Printing Company in Omaha.

Also, I was surrounded with Helen and my friend Bertha Griggs both who had inner speaking from God, and he surrounded me with other women who had the gift.

This was important for me because when I was in the convent, I had my first mystical experience and it frightened me. I was standing in what we called the great room by the long table with chairs that seated all the postulants and all the novices. I was turning pages in a picture book of ancient churches. In one picture I saw a procession of nuns going into the pews. I was immediately in that church. I felt the presence of God. I was so frightened by the fire and intensity of His love that I felt I would be consumed by it. I immediately came back to the present and I was still standing.

Until lately, I have not told anyone else about this experience except my college friend Bob Winters. His immediate reaction was "neat." I loved God and all that entailed, but I wasn't sure I wanted to be that close to Him, and that all changed in 1982. In 1982 at the first healing Mass my mother and I attended, when we heard Father Bill speak, we both knew God talks to him. After Mass was over, Father would talk and announce the healings of people in the Church. The people would come forward and own their healings.

Then Father Bill would have each of us come up and kneel at the communion railing where we knelt during Mass to receive Communion, and in this case for a special blessing and a healing. He would bless each one of us, and often he gave us special messages or prophecies from Jesus. It seems unbelievable but it was real. I would kneel next to my mother on one side and Helen on the other. I would hear and remember their messages and immediately go back to our pew and write them down for them. I particularly remembered four of the messages I wrote down for Helen from Jesus. She saved them. I saved the two messages about my two civil rights law cases.

The first message for me was in late November 1985. I had been ill and had just gotten an order from the Federal Court that a case I had been

71

handling since 1982 was set for trial the first week in January, 1986. That case, as I told you before, was Crystal Chambers v. The Omaha Girls Club et al, the sex, race and pregnancy discrimination case I filed under the 1964 Civil Rights Act and the 1978 Pregnancy Discrimination Act for my 21 year old black, single and pregnant arts and craft teacher Crystal Chambers. I told Father that the Club fired Crystal because she was single and pregnant and black and told her bosses that she was glad she was being promoted to full time status with health insurance because she was pregnant and was going to raise her child. She was forced to go on welfare.

I told him that another black, single pregnant employee who was given notice of termination was allowed to keep her job because she had an abortion; the Club at trial claimed they didn't force her to have an abortion but the Club by its actions made having an abortion a condition for continued employment. The message I got through Father was: "You will speak in a loud voice and the words you will speak will be Mine, and you will be heard." The message went on: "My justice is a two edge sword."

In that one month before the trial, I assembled the best trial team of two additional lawyers, Omaha lawyer Ed Fogarty, my friend since college days, and DeKalb, Illinois attorney Ed Diedrich. Ed Diedrich won a similar single pregnant teacher role model case for his white client Jeanne Echmann who had been raped. As I told you, the case was made into a movie titled: 'Cast the First Stone.' Ed brought his two law clerks, and my friend Midge Newman and her friend Sharene Schwartz were our paralegals. My fourteen year old daughters and their friend Isabelle Taylor were our clerks.

Crystal's trial started in January of 1986 and went past the Martin Luther King holiday. I previously told you about the book I published in 2007 about Crystal's case. Chapter 9 of that book is titled: "The Loud Voice." It is about the prophecy "You will speak in a loud voice and the words that you speak will be Mine and you will be heard" and all the national publicity we got in 1986 on the case as I noted earlier: National Public Radio twice, the *New York Times* Sunday edition, *Newsweek*, *The New York Daily News*, *In These Times*, and on *Donahue* a daily talk show hosted by Phil Donahue, as well as in the *Omaha World Herald* and the *Lincoln Journal Star* in Lincoln, Nebraska.

The *Omaha World Herald* did not run the *The New York Times* article, but the *Lincoln Journal Star* did. Dave Thomson of the *Omaha World*

Sundance and Cherokee Moon

Herald called me about the *Times* article in the *Lincoln Journal Star*. I immediately went out to the news stand and bought it. I got a phone call that day from Gail Stenberg of the *Donahue* show. Phil Donahue read the *New York Times* Sunday piece and wanted us on his show.

I got to co-produce the Phil Donahue show by selecting the other formerly single pregnant teachers and their attorneys from a file I kept. The other mothers brought their children with them. I didn't think we were supposed to so Crystal didn't bring her daughter Ruthie. Phil Donahue and his New York audience were so nice to us. It was such a relief from the treatment of us by the *Omaha World Herald* which endorsed the Girls Club discrimination.

The legal team I assembled in December, 1985, thought the "Loud Voice" prophecy meant we were going to win but it turned out it was about all the favorable national publicity. In 2003, black radio talk show host Tom Joyner featured Crystal and her case in his thirty minute segment "Little Known Black Heroes." By coincidence my daughter Mary Kay and I were in the car and screamed when we heard him talking about Crystal we were so excited. Unfortunately his show was not broadcast in Omaha, but I called Crystal and told her about it.

Again, the second prophecy I received from the Lord through Father Bill was about my 1988 trial which started that summer in the case of EBA, the Employee Betterment Association v. the City of Omaha et al for six city workers. The case eventually was captioned Avis Linstrom v. The City of Omaha et al. The prophecy was: "All the people involved will turn against you." I had told Father that I was starting a major civil rights case for a number of city employees who alleged discrimination. As I told you before, Father announced: "All the people involved will turn against you." I was stunned. Years later I told Father Bill that I didn't know that Jesus was a lawyer. He smiled.

In July of 1988, I knelt next to Helen and went back to the pew to write down what the Lord had said to her through Father Bill. Helen just sent me copies of the envelopes I wrote on. That first message read: "The Lord knows that you are suffering and that you have been crowned with thorns such as His. But he wants you to know that it will be lifted."

She also sent me the message I wrote down for her on April 18, 1989: "I see your sacrifices. Always seek refuge in me."

73

Sundance and Cherokee Moon

On January 9, 1991, I wrote what the Lord said to her through Father Bill: "My daughter your prayers for peace have been so pleasing to me. They have made a difference."

February 13, 1991 the Lord said: "Helen, my daughter, I am so pleased with your prayers for peace, because of your efforts days will be taken from the length of the war." The civil war that would break out later in Yugoslavia was the war the Lord was referring to.

In an undated message for Helen, I wrote: "The Lord will bless your works. The Lord will fill your purse to overflowing. And when your life comes to an end Our Lord will welcome you home with open arms."

I was unable to retrieve my mother's messages from the Lord when she died because I was living in Kansas City at the time and couldn't help going through her things to save them.
.
Back in September of 1988, I got an inner speaking that the Blessed Mother wanted to come to Omaha but that she wanted to be invited. I told my friend City Clerk Mary Galligan Cornett about this, and she told me that the Mayor had just given several keys to the city to a group of individuals from Russia. "Why don't you get a key to the city from the Mayor for the Blessed Mother?" she said. She had me call the Mayor's office to order a plaque with the key to the city for the Blessed Mother. When his secretary asked me who the key to the city was for, I told her just to make it out for "Mary."

When the plaque didn't come, Mary had me call the Mayor's office again. His secretary explained that the Mayor needed "Mary's" last name. I told her: "The Blessed Virgin Mary." Three days later I picked up the plaque with the key to the city and the inscription to "The Blessed Virgin Mary" on it. I was also given an envelope with six small keys for the six young visionaries. Mayor Walter Calinger was a law classmate of mine and a friend. And we both clerked for attorney Ben Wall, and we both were elected to the Omaha City Council, he after me. Walt is Croatian American. The people in Medjugorje all speak Croatian. He is also a Catholic like me.

I made an appointment with Father Bill at the end of September before we left for Medjugorje. His assistant let me in and told me that Father was in his office. I stood in his office doorway. When he saw me he immediately

74

got up from his chair, smiled, and rushed over to where I was standing. He took my hands in his and said: "The Lord is speaking to you!" I smiled back and said: "Yes!" He wasn't asking me, he was telling me. Father was affirming my own belief as to who was talking to me internally. I followed him to his desk and sat down in a chair in front of the desk. I told Father about the first message I got from Our Lord. He advised me to consult with him or another priest for discernment of Our Lord's messages.

I told Father that my mother and I were going on a pilgrimage in October to Medjugorje with Father Thomas Halley, S.J. as our chaplain on the trip. Father Bill told me that Father Halley was very close to the Blessed Mother. I encouraged Father Bill to go there himself. When my mother and I got back, I learned that Father Bill was taking a group including Helen to Medjugorje that same month after we returned.

While Father Whelan said Mass for his group in the chapel next to the main altar in St. James Church in Medjugorje where some of the apparitions took place, he had a mystical experience seeing the Blessed Mother walk behind each of the pilgrims from Omaha putting her hands on their shoulders and blessing each one. He told everyone what she was doing as she went from person to person. I heard about it from Helen first and later Father described to me how mystical and beautiful the experience was.

Before we left for Medjugorje, I saw a very small article in *The New York Times* that Martin Sheen was in Medjugorje. Martin Sheen is a famous actor who played President Bartlett in the hit television series *West Wing*. I excitedly said to the Lord: "You want a movie made about Medjugorje, don't you. And you want Martin Sheen to play Father Jozo (the priest who befriended and protected the young visionaries from the Communist government), don't you?" The response I got was 'Yes.' I immediately typed up this message and put it in my purse. I knew I had to give it to someone but I didn't know who. I would tell Father Halley about it when we were in Medjugorje.

The rest of the pilgrims in our group had a direct flight from Omaha to Chicago. We had joined the pilgrimage late, so my mother and I had to fly to Kansas City and then to Chicago to meet up with the rest of the group and Father Halley. I carried my purse with me and a royal blue imitation leather zippered bag with the Key to the City for the Blessed Mother and the six smaller keys in it. The purse and the bag went through security without causing the alarm to go off. I mentioned the fact to my mother. "What do you think that means?" she asked. I didn't know.

The same thing happened going through security in Kansas City to our flight to Chicago. When we arrived in Chicago, I showed the plaque to Father Halley and told him about the message I got that the Blessed Mother wanted to come to Omaha but that she wanted to be asked and how I got the Key to the City for the Blessed Mother and six small metal keys from Mayor Walter Calinger of Croatian descent and that my bag with the metal Key to the City in it and the six small metal keys went through security in Omaha and Kansas City without triggering the alarms. See the picture of the Key to the City at the end of this book, I hope it uploads.

Father Halley told me: "Mary Kay, the Blessed Mother is protecting it and will protect it all the way to Medjugorje." Father had me show the plaque to the others and the six smaller keys and tell them how they went through security in Omaha and again in Kansas City, Missouri without incident. We all watched the bag go through Chicago to New York, New York to Frankfurt, Germany and from Frankfurt, Germany to Dubrovnik and through security in Dubrovnik, Yugoslavia. The bag with the wood and metal plaque and the large metal key on it and the six small metal keys passed through security in six cities and in three countries. I worried about Dubrovnik because we were in a Communist country, but Father Halley was right. The Blessed Mother protected our gift the whole way to Medjugorje. And she would accept our invitation to come to Omaha.

As I mentioned earlier, Our Lady is called Our Lady Queen of Peace of Medjugorje. Her purpose for the apparitions is to bring everyone to her Son, Our Lord Jesus Christ and to bring peace to the world. People of all nations came and continue to come to be in her presence for spiritual healings even today, and to receive special graces for their lives. Some receive physical healings as well. It was often told to us that while you are in Medjugorje you experience this heavenly feeling of joy that can last up to six months after you leave. That is another of the blessings you get from answering Our Lady's call to come.

A chartered bus was waiting for us at the airport in Dubrovnik. It was about a three hour trip to Medjugorje. The sun was out and the country side was still green and beautiful. We sang spiritual songs including the Ave Maria and said the rosary together out loud. Father had a microphone

Sundance and Cherokee Moon

and he led us in song and in the rosary. He told us that these days in Medjugorje would be a deeply spiritual time.

Like the priest at St. Margaret Mary's, Father told us of all the sites we would see: St. James Church for the American and International Masses and Our Lady's apparitions to Ivan, Apparition Hill where the Blessed Mother first appeared and often still appears, Mt. Krezivak or Cross Mountain where she also appears, and we would have an opportunity to go to confession, walk through the vineyards to see the homes of the visionaries, visit with Ivan and Vicka, both of whom still have daily apparitions from Our Lady, and that we would be staying with Vicka's family.

Marija also still has daily apparitions but she was married and living in Italy with her husband at the time. These three visionaries still have daily apparitions to date. Mirjana was given the ten secrets for the world which Our Lady will reveal through her, and she has an apparition and a message for the world from Our Lady on the 2nd and 25th day of each month. The others still get apparitions on specials days.

We made one rest stop on the way at an inn. At the inn they served the most delicious non-carbonated fresh peach drink made from peaches grown in the area. We were all pleased. When the people in the inn learned that we were on our way to Medjugorje, they shouted their blessings to us as we left. The closer we got, the more excited we got.

When we arrived in Medjugorje, it was night, a very dark night. The bus driver did not take us to Vicka's family home in the heart of the village to stay, but instead took us to a place farther away. Father Halley was upset about this, but what could he do. Six of us stayed in one home with Rosa and her husband George as our hosts. My mother and my friend Mary Ann and her two children Benjamin and Juliette and another friend Marie and I stayed with Rosa and George. The rest of the group including Father Halley stayed in an inn across the street. We were all tired but at the same time exhilarated at finally being in Medjugorje.

In our packet from the Intercessors, we received a sheet of paper with the September 25, 1988, monthly message for the world from Our Lady:

Dear children, today I am calling all of you without exception to the way of holiness. Pray that you may more and more comprehend it

77

and in that way, you will be able by your life to bear witness for God. Dear children, I am blessing you and I intercede for you to God so that your way and your witness may be a complete one and a joy for God. Thank you for having   responded to my call.

After dinner, Father Halley had us all assemble on the bus for a ride down to the foot of Apparition Hill. He had us climb the rocks half way up the hill to the spot where Ivan was to hold his Tuesday evening prayer meeting. The rocks were muddy and slippery because it was drizzling. Father explained that the prayer group was originally started by Marija and Ivan on Mondays and Fridays. But when Marija married and moved to Italy, Ivan carried on the prayer group himself. Pilgrims joined him for the continuous saying of the rosary. The Blessed Mother would appear to him and all prayers would stop and the crowd would be silent while she appeared to him. We learned from others while we climbed the hill that the prayer group had been cancelled because of the rain.

Years later in one of the books titled *Words from Heaven, the Messages from Medjugorje*, the message of Our Lady for the next week October 17, 1988, was:

> Dear children, tonight your Mother is happy, joyful together with you. I would like to extend happiness to you. I would like to give you love, so you can bring this love and spread it to others. I would like to give you peace so that you can give this peace to others, so you can give this peace especially to families where hatred exists. I would like you to encourage others to renew this prayer. Your Mother will help you.

When we got home that first night, we all went straight to bed. I was in a deep sleep when I was awakened by an exterior voice after midnight. I was told to kneel down and to pray for everyone I came to pray for. "But if I do, I will be exhausted in the morning," I said. "Trust me, you will be rested," the voice said. I crawled out of bed and got on my knees to pray for the people on the list of 500 names and prayed for all the people on the list, one at a time. And in the morning, I felt totally refreshed.

I prepared my list with the names of my parents, my seven siblings and their families, my grandparents, my aunts and uncles and cousins and their families, and friends from the women's rights movement, the civil rights movement, other friends, lawyer colleagues, judges, nuns, priests, politicians, and all the names of the people who worked on my successful City Council campaign. The names of my supporters were captured on large file cards and maintained in a yellow, wooden file box by my dear friend and campaign volunteer retired Colonel Quinn Smith. Quinn stayed close to my girls and me after the campaign. All three of us cherish his friendship.

In the morning we went in cabs to St. James Church, the church of the apparitions, for the daily English speaking Mass. We got there in time to get seats and to say two complete rosaries out loud before Mass began. Father Phillip Pavich, an American Franciscan priest, said this daily American Mass. When he learned of the apparitions in Medjugorje, he came there to minister to all the American pilgrims. In his sermon after the gospel, Father told the story of the beginning of the apparitions to the six young people and how they fled to this church for protection when the Communist government officials tried to arrest them and tried to keep the villagers from the hill where Our Lady first appeared. The church was full for Mass and the Communion lines were long. A number of visiting priests assisted Father Pavich in saying the Mass and in giving out Holy Communion.

After Mass, Father Halley secured transportation for us so we could go to Apparition Hill and climb it. Unlike last night's dark and rainy sky, today we climbed the hill in sunshine and with a beautiful blue sky. Back in Omaha at the Medjugorje Masses sponsored by the Intercessors of the Lamb, we were told to bring pictures of our loved ones and to place them in the bushes as we climbed the hill, and that the Blessed Mother would bless them. I brought pictures of my daughters, and my mother brought a family photo of her and all eight of us children, my siblings' spouses and all our children and a picture of my dad who died in 1968. We put our pictures in bushes going up the hill.

Father Halley had me bring the plaque with the Key to the City for the Blessed Mother and the six smaller metal keys and together we laid them on the ledge by the largest cross. (See picture of Father Halley and me placing the plaque and the keys near the cross marking the Blessed Mother's first apparitions. I hope it uploads). Father spoke words of praise to the Blessed Mother and told her that we are inviting her and the visionaries to Omaha.

Sundance and Cherokee Moon

Then, Father led us in the glorious mysteries of the rosary (the Resurrection, the Ascension of Our Lord into heaven, the Descent of the Holy Spirit on the apostles, the Assumption of the Blessed Mother into heaven and the coronation of the Blessed Mother as Queen of heaven and earth). After that Father told us to take some of the small stones and handfuls of the soil in the plastic containers he had us bring because the Blessed Mother blessed the stones and the soil of the hill and she encouraged people to take them as blessed items.

Once down the hill, and it was more difficult coming down than going up, Father took us through the grape orchards to the home of Ivan. While we were in Medjugorje, Ivan had his daily apparition in the choir loft in St. James Church. Father knocked on Ivan's door and he came out to greet us with his interpreter. Years later, all the visionaries could speak English, but not now. Father told Ivan that we brought him a plaque with a key to the City of Omaha for the Blessed Mother, along with six smaller keys for each of the visionaries, to invite the Blessed Mother to Omaha and the visionaries as well.

Ivan told us that he would present the plaque with the Key to the City, and the smaller keys, to the Blessed Mother when she appeared to him at 4:30 p.m. before the International Mass. We were thrilled. It was a pure collective act of faith and obedience on our part to invite the Blessed Mother with the visionaries to come to Omaha because the Communist government was not allowing the visionaries to leave Medjugorje at that time, but Our Lord told me to invite her. We also knew that the government would not even allow Mother Teresa of Calcutta, India, to come into Yugoslavia because she was Albanian.

When we left Ivan, Father Halley suggested that we go back to the church because on the far side of the church, several priests from all over the world were hearing confessions. Going to the Sacrament of Confession in Medjugorje was recommended as part of the spiritual experience. When I became a single mother, I left the Catholic Church because of its discrimination against the children of unmarried parents. "Illegitimate" children were barred from the priesthood and religious life, and the church in Rome kept track of these births by country. The Church was obsessed with these families. There was another reason I never sent my children to Catholic schools.

When I was a social worker for Douglas County, one day I had to take the intake application of a young single mother. Because she lived with her older sister, her sister's caseworker had to be present too. He verbally attacked this young woman and accused her of being immoral. She was in tears he was so harsh. When he left, I told her that we are not here to condemn you. We are only here to help you. I reported the incident to the director and he did nothing about it. He told me that the Hispanic man was Catholic and Catholics cannot tolerate illegitimacy. I never forgot that incident.

The only time my girls were subjected to discrimination in the Public Schools was by a Catholic teacher who had just come from Des Moines where she heard Pope John Paul II speak, so much for "love thy neighbor." This teacher was punishing Elizabeth because she was born to a single mother. I sat in Elizabeth's classroom one day under the open classroom policy for parents and the teacher even did it even in front of me. I called my eighth teacher Sister Mary Teresita (later she was able to use her first name as her sister name and she was known as Sister Mary Helen) and sobbed about what that teacher was doing to my daughter. She had me go to the principal and have him remove Elizabeth from that classroom immediately. He did.

Mary Kay's teacher Mrs. Shearer agreed to take Elizabeth in her classroom along with Mary Kay. The principal James Freeman, a black man who had marched with Martin Luther King in Selma, Alabama, broke the district rule that twins cannot be in the same class together. Elizabeth's grades went back up to all A's from the D's that teacher gave her. That other teacher so harassed her that her grades went down to D's. This was an example of how a bad teacher can destroy a student. Tragically, Mrs. Schearer, the good teacher, died two years later from cancer. What a good woman she was. She was married with children.

During those thirteen years that I was away from the Catholic Church, I also suffered a dark period of doubt of the existence of God called the dark night of the soul. What I experienced is called agnosticism. But I never stopped praying. My prayer was: "Oh God, if there is a God, please help me." I only started going back to the Catholic Church in 1982, as I previously related, after Helen and my friend Clare separately told me about Father Bill's healing Masses and services and my mother and I began going to them once a week.

At the same time that I was going to Father Bill's weekly healing Mass, I was going every Sunday with my friend Mary Cornett to Trinity Episcopal

Sundance and Cherokee Moon

Cathedral with Father John Fricke. I wanted to join a church that believed as I do in the real presence of Jesus in Communion. Both faiths had the Sacraments of the Mass and Holy Communion. I didn't know which one I would join. Father Fricke died of cancer the next year and I became a full time Catholic still continuing with Father Bill's weekly healing Mass with mother and going to church on Sundays.

In 1982, as I earlier reported, I was suffering severe grief over the death of three men important in my life who died in the same thirty day period. I was so grief stricken that I couldn't work for six months and during that time my long time friend Ed Fogarty took over my practice. In my grief, I developed bulimia. After passing out once, I struggled to stop the vomiting, but it took longer to stop the compulsive eating to fill that terrible void, to fill that long tunnel of emptiness inside of me that I imagined went all the way down to China. I desperately needed professional help.

There was only one program in Omaha at the time for people suffering anorexia and bulimia and it was for teenagers. And beside, I no longer had health insurance to pay for therapy. So when Clare and Helen separately told me about Father Bill's healing Masses and healing services, I decided I would ask God through Father to heal me. As I reported earlier, the first healing Mass my mother and I attended, we both knew instantly that God talks to Father Bill. We attended Father's Masses for nearly ten years until he was transferred to St. Augustine's parish in Schuyler, Nebraska.

But when my third friend was dying, a man who had encouraged me to go to law school and who was my mentor and beloved friend, I got a psychic knowing that he was dying. I had stopped driving a few weeks earlier when he was so ill because one evening when I was thinking about how near death he was, I forgot to put the emergency brake on my Volvo. As the car started to roll down the steep driveway, I jumped into the car trying to stop it. The car plunged across the street and then it stopped suddenly.

I got out of the car to see who or what could have stopped it from going up my neighbor's lawn across the street and who or what prevented me from smashing into the front of his house in my car. There was no one there. There was nothing to stop the car. But someone with super human force had stopped the car. I felt the jolt pushing the car forward. This was the first time I survived death in an automobile, the second being later at Lake

Sundance and Cherokee Moon

City, Iowa, after my pilgrimage to Medjugorje in 1988. "God must not be through with me yet." I gratefully said to myself.

I was forty-six when I went with Father Halley and my mother and thirty-three others to Medjugorje. My mother at the time was sixty-nine. She lived to eighty-seven and I am still surprised to be alive at seventy-three. The last time I saw Father Halley after my sixteenth summer, was years later when my Uncle Ed Furay died. My Uncle Ed and my Aunt Jeanie were my godparents and they let me live with them the last four months of my pregnancy in 1969 in Cinnaminson, N.J. and for four months afterward till I moved with my babies to Washington, D.C. to work for the Robert F. Kennedy Memorial.

As I previously noted, my late father James F. Green had been the working Nebraska co-chairman of both John Kennedy's and Robert Kennedy's Presidential campaigns. My father died suddenly of grief over Robert Kennedy's assassination eight days after Robert Kennedy died. Fred Dutton, one of Robert Kennedy's lieutenants, worked with my dad on the campaign and as director of the Robert F. Kennedy Memorial, he hired me.

My Uncle Ed was a descendant of the Creighton family who founded Creighton Prep Jesuit High School for boys (my grandfather Pat Phelan graduated from Prep as did my father, my two brothers and two of my nephews) and Creighton College, a Jesuit college. Years later Creighton became a university.

My father and mother and my three maternal aunts and two of my uncles went to Creighton in the 1940's. Father Halley made note of my uncle's connection to Creighton and the founding family in his eulogy for my uncle. My dad and my uncle Dick Coughlin graduated from law school there. All of my siblings except one when to Creighton University, and she and four others of us went to Creighton University Law School along with two cousins and four neighbors all inspired by my dad.

The 1988 trip to Medjugorje for my mother and I, started a wonderful friendship with Father Halley, this holy Irish leprechaun of a priest, which would last until his death after fifty years of being ordained as a priest. I eventually learned a few years before he died that Father had the gift of bi-location, meaning that he could be in two places at the same time like some of the saints. One time he was at the Saturday night prayer group at St. Margaret Mary's Church in Omaha, (he was the chaplain of that group) and at the same time, as Father Bill verified, Father Halley was in California with him. The other time I know of was when he attended all three days of his former altar boy's trial. Father told me he only attended the trial one day, but his former altar boy and his mother both told me that father was there all three days. His bi-located self was there the last two days.

Witnesses at that prayer group said that the Father Halley who was there that night looked younger than he usually looked. I was able to go to the Saturday night prayer group for a couple of years. Years after my inner speaking or inner locutions started, I asked Father Halley: "Why is the Lord speaking to me? I am a liberal?" "Jesus was a liberal, Mary Kay," Father replied. When I thought about what Jesus taught, love of God and love of neighbor and forgiveness, and mercy, his teachings were revolutionary. His teachings about love and forgiveness and mercy are still revolutionary even now. Too many people and nations ignore these commandments.

It has been recently reported that the visionary Vicka has the gift of bi-location like Father Halley. Earlier she was given the gift of healing like Father Halley and Father Whelan. Vicka still has daily apparitions from the Blessed Mother.

When Father Halley said to me that Jesus was a liberal, it hit home to me that the Lord truly loves us all, liberal me included: single, never married mother, liberal Democrat, plaintiffs' civil rights attorney, Catholic feminist and a woman who prays. Pope Francis embodies the principals of Our Lord in loving and welcoming all peoples and in preaching love of God, our neighbors and mercy and forgiveness just like Jesus.

If you are not a liberal, don't shut the book. I pray every day and pray together when I am able to attend Mass at Our Lady of the Presentation Parish in Lees Summit, MO, and pray the rosary afterward with people who are liberal, moderate, conservative and super conservative. We care about one another, worship the same God at Mass, pray the rosary together and socialize together.

Back in Medjugorje, when we reached the far side of St. James Church to go to confession, the scene reminded me of the World War II movies showing priests kneeling and hearing confessions near the battle field full of metal helmeted soldiers kneeling in front of them while guns went off nearby.

There was no battle field in Medjugorje in 1988, but war would break out in Yugoslavia later and by terms of the negotiated peace agreement the country would be divided into three states. This agreement was called the Dayton Peace Accord negotiated by NATO Commander U.S. General Wesley Clark. Miraculously Medjugorje was not bombed, but the village hosted hundreds of refuges from the war.
The priests that day we waited for confession didn't kneel but sat on small wooden stools with pilgrims kneeling in front of them to recite their confessions. There were rows and rows of benches for pilgrims to wait their turns at confession.

In 2005, when someone above pressed the print button of my brain for two full weeks of automatic writing, which resulted in my book *Women of Courage*, I travelled with my daughter Elizabeth to Wright Patterson Airbase where she was attending a conference as part of her job as a Navy civilian employee. In the booklet we received when checking in at the motel on base where we were staying, it had a page noting that at this motel, the Dayton Peace Accord ending the war in Yugoslavia was negotiated by NATO Commander General Wesley Clark. The next morning while Elizabeth was at her conference, I found the room where the negotiations and the signing of the Accord took place. There was a plaque on the entrance to the room immortalizing this historical happening. This peace accord was one of the events that the Blessed Mother had all of us praying for.

In 1988, at the side of Saint James Church in Medjugorje, my mother and I sat on a bench with young Irish women pilgrims from Northern Ireland praying for peace there. These young women looked just like me and my mother when she was young. Our family is Irish American on both my mother's and my father's side. My mother's father, my grandfather Patrick Joseph Phelan came to America from Ireland with his parents when he was twelve years old. Both of my grandmothers' families and my grandfather Green's family came over earlier than that.

We told the young Irish women that we prayed for peace in Northern Ireland every Tuesday at our healing services back in Omaha, and that we prayed for peace in the Middle East as well.

Sundance and Cherokee Moon

My mother, who went there twice, and all my siblings have been to Ireland. I hope to get there one day to visit with my daughters and grandchildren. Meeting these young Irish women was almost as exciting for me as when in about 1985, I met future Pulitzer Peace Prize winner John Hume, the leader of the Northern Ireland Catholics, who traveled with Ian Paisley, the leader of the Protestants, on a trade mission to America promoting jobs in Northern Ireland. I met both John Hume and Ian Paisley at a party in Washington, D.C. thrown for the delegation by the owners of the Sheraton Hotel chain.

John Hume and I had a conversation about the possible use of American civil rights laws for the situation in Northern Ireland. I spent about twenty minutes with him. David Trimble, first minister of Northern Ireland, and John Hume later shared the Nobel Peace Prize in 1998 for their negotiations of a peace treaty with former U.S. Senator George Mitchell. Senator Mitchell was sent to Ireland by President Bill Clinton to help negotiate what became the Good Friday Peace Accord settling the "troubles," the killings in Northern Ireland between the Catholics and the Protestants there.

Recently the CBS television network show *60 Minutes* featured a segment on the still total segregation of the Catholics and Protestants in Ireland with gates locking their communities at night. While there is no violence, the harsh feelings still prevail.

I went to confession that day in Medjugorje to a black bishop from Africa. He had spoken at an English Mass. While growing up in Omaha in the 50's and 60's there was only one black priest, Father Cunningham, a Jesuit priest at Creighton University. And the sister's of Mercy, the order who taught me in grade school and high school and was the order that I entered in 1960, only had one black sister. As I noted earlier, I stayed only a school year in the convent. One of the students in our high school, a young black student and the only black student in our Catholic girls school at the time, entered the Sisters of Mercy. I don't know if she stayed with the order.

After my Confession (a Sacrament of the Catholic Church like the Mass, Baptism, Confirmation, Holy Orders, Matrimony, and the Sacrament of Healing), and it was a joyful confession (and years since my last Confession), I saw that my mother was finished too.

86

Sundance and Cherokee Moon

We decided to walk behind the back of the church so we could enter the entrance on the other side. All of a sudden my mother grabbed my arm. She was looking up at the sun. I looked up too. The sun had a black circle over it with a white edge all around it. In Omaha, we had been told about the Miracle of the Sun but were never told about the black sun.

The Miracle of the Sun in Medjugorje is similar to the "Dancing Sun" in Fatima, but it still exists since 1981 in Medjugorje and else where. In Medjugorje, as I previously noted, the round sun is either gold, gold-orange or white like a communion host is covering the sun and with various colors pulsating around it. Unlike the sun in Fatima where 100,000 thousand people (according to first person accounts) saw it at one time, in Medjugorje not all the people see it at the same time.

All of a sudden, the black sun started to spin, and it plunged to the earth near us spinning, and just as rapidly it spun back up in the sky. My mother and I looked at each other in disbelief. We were stunned. "Oh my God!" I exclaimed! We just kept looking at each other. It was such a personal experience that we didn't tell anyone. Years later in March of 2011 at Caritas I learned that other people have seen the miracle of the black sun in Medjugorje too.

Caritas is a community near Birmingham, Alabama, dedicated to publishing Our Lady's messages and spreading them in book form and online (Medugorje.com, Mej.com) throughout the world. The members of the community also take people to Medjugorje for pilgrimages. I learned there that other people have seen the black sun. When I told Helen about what I learned at Caritas, she said that she had also seen the black sun during her pilgrimage led by Father Whelan in October of 1988, but, she hadn't talked about it either. I went to Caritas because the visionary Marija was going to be there for a week and the Blessed Mother would be appearing there to her and we would be present.

Back at Medjugorje, the church was packed that afternoon for the International Mass. My mother and I got in but it was standing room only. We were in a spot where we could see the altar and all the priests and we could turn around and look up at the choir loft where the apparition to Ivan would take place.

Ivan came into the choir loft and everyone turned to see him. He was standing at the railing and looking down at all the people. Suddenly a wide gold ribbon rolled from his shoulder and across the congregation to me. It was a vision of a beautiful gold ribbon, and I didn't know the meaning of this phenomenon until a few years later, but after seeing the black spinning sun and the Miracle of the Sun, the miraculous seemed to be the norm in Medjugorje.

It would be a few years before I would understand the connection between Ivan and me. I would receive an inner speaking or inner locution in 1989 that the Blessed Mother was coming to Omaha with Ivan to Immaculate Conception Church (where Father Bill had been reassigned). My friend Rosemary, who had joined us in Medjugorje from Europe with her mother, sister and aunt, was with me when we saw a grey cloud travel from 24th and Martha street down 24th street past Immaculate Conception Church several blocks to Vinton Street and back down 25th Street in South Omaha. I mentioned to Rosemary that in Medjugorje we learned that the Blessed Mother always appeared with her feet on a grey cloud.

We had originally believed there was a fire up on 24th Street, even worried that smoke was coming from the church, but when we got up the hill to 24th Street, we saw that it was this grey cloud about fifteen feet above Rosemary's car. We followed the grey cloud, which was just ahead of us, as far as we could. I got an inner speaking at that time that the Blessed Mother was coming to Omaha with Ivan at Immaculate Conception Church. I told Rosemary immediately. Years later she would make a sworn statement or deposition under oath on these events. I still have that deposition.

Rosemary and I went to the church rectory where Father lived and had his office and found him. I told him about the message and that Our Lady would be with Ivan at his church. I asked him what we were supposed to do, and he answered: "We must just stay in prayer for the Blessed Mother will let us know." He told us not to tell anyone.

Two years later in December, 1991, I got a phone call from Helen, who was assisting Father. She told me that Father Whelan wanted me to know that the Blessed Mother and Ivan were coming to Omaha, December 7th, the observation day that year of the feast of the Immaculate Conception. The feast day December 8th fell on a Sunday so Saturday the 7th was celebrated as the holy day.

Sundance and Cherokee Moon

I talked to Father and asked him if I should call the Intercessors of the Lamb, where Ivan and his interpreter would be staying, and tell them that Ivan and the Blessed Mother were supposed to be at Immaculate Conception Church. Father said: "We must let Our Lady make the selection." Our Lady appeared to Ivan at the Intercessors of the Lamb at 4:30 p.m. Rosemary and her mother Teresa were there in the next room, but her mother who speaks many languages was given the gift of hearing the conversation between Our Lady and Ivan.

Later in the evening, the Mass was held with Ivan's talk at Immaculate Conception Church. I tell all about this service later in the book. I have a VHS copy of the Mass and the service with Ivan that day and audio cassettes.

But back to Medjugorje in 1988, at 4:30 p.m., all of a sudden Ivan knelt. Our Lady was appearing to him. Time seemed to stop until he rose again. Before the apparition, we said two rosaries and the priest saying the Mass told us that the Blessed Mother would bless each of us during her apparition to Ivan and bless all the rosaries and metals and religious items we brought to Mass. The International Mass was always said in Croatian unlike the American Mass we attended earlier at 10:00 a.m.

The Communion service took longer than the rest of the Mass because there were so many people receiving Communion inside the church and outdoors. There were speakers outdoors to accommodate all the people who could not fit in the church.

On another evening, mother and I were not able to get into the church, so we stood outdoors by the front doors. Large stained glass windows were above the doors where the choir loft was. When Our Lady appeared in the choir loft, hundreds of birds filled those stained glass windows and flew away instantly when Our Lady went back to heaven. We witnessed this beautiful tribute by the birds. Being in Medjugorje with all the miracles, we all were filled with tremendous joy and feelings of peace. By tradition, as I noted, these extraordinary feelings usually last for six months after people go back home.

We all saw the Miracle of the Sun the next day after meeting Father Jozo, the priest who protected the young visionaries from the Communist government those early years. Father served eighteen months in prison because of his efforts to protect the children. After his release, Father was assigned a new parish some distance from Medjugorje. At one point because the young visionaries were so fearful for Father Jozo, the Blessed Mother let them see him in jail to show them that he was all right.

I previously told you about seeing the small article in the *New York Times* newspaper that Martin Sheen was in Medjugorje right before we were there. Father Halley encouraged me to bring the paper I wrote the message on that God wanted a movie made about Medjugorje and that he wanted Martin Sheen to play Father Jozo. I brought the paper to give to Father Jozo after his talk to us through his interpreter. I went up to the communion rail where Father Jozo was standing with his interpreter and handed the paper to him and told him what I was handing him. Father smiled at me and gave the message to his interpreter who read it to Father Jozo. A few years later the movie 'Gospa: The Miracle of Medjugorje' came out in VHS (I have an original copy). "Gospa" means mother. Martin Sheen played Father Jozo in the movie.

I don't know if Martin Sheen and Father Jozo were discussing the film back in 1988, and that my message was just a confirmation or not. But the movie was very good and brought back memories of our pilgrimage. The movie is out now in DVD, and you can buy it or rent it from Amazon.com. It covers the first few years of the apparitions. I ordered it on Amazon.com as well as the 'Miracle of Fatima' and the Academy Award winning movie 'The Song of Bernadette' about the apparitions of the Blessed Mother to St. Bernadette in Lourdes, France, and 'Therese.' the movie about the life of St. Therese, the Little Flower of Jesus and the Holy Face.

These movies are about the three major apparitions of the Blessed Mother: the first two series of apparitions at Lourdes, France, ('Song of Bernadette,') and at Fatima, Portugal, ('Miracle at Fatima,') are approved by the Catholic Church, and the continuous apparitions related to Medjugorje for the last thirty-three years are now being studied by the Church.

Usually the approval for apparitions is studied and made after the apparitions end, but the apparitions in Medjugorje are being studied while the Blessed Mother continues to appear. The author Steve Berry writes about these three apparition sites in his popular book *The Third Secret*, a fact-based novel with true accounts of the three apparition sites and the young people the Blessed Mother appears to.

Sundance and Cherokee Moon

Recently in October, 2013, a statue of the Blessed Mother owned by Vicka for over thirty years became luminescent, surrounded in pure light. So many thousands of people came through her home to see the glowing statue that Vicka's brother carried it into St. James Church so that everyone including the villagers and the pilgrims could see this miracle. The Vatican commission sent observers to document this continuing phenomenon.

Let's go back to our third day in Medjugorje. (I wander like an old Irish story teller.) As I told you previously, the third day we climbed Mt. Krizevak after the American Mass. In the 1930's the villagers built a huge stone cross at the top of the mountain. They carried bags of cement up the mountain together with water and all the materials they needed to build the cross. This was a beautiful day for us to climb for the weather was perfect, the sun was shinning, the sky was light blue and white fluffy clouds filled the sky.

Father Halley brought his Mass vestments or garments, some wine, a little water and the Communion hosts for Communion to be distributed to us during the Mass he said for us after they were consecrated. (See the pictures of Father Halley saying Mass on Mt. Krizevak. Hopefully it uploaded.) Climbing down the mountain, just as climbing up it, was difficult, but people helped each other. It was the tradition of the villagers to climb the mountain barefoot. It was amazing to watch them rapidly move their feet on those rocks and stones up and down the mountain. I should note that a Catholic priest can say two Masses a day and Catholics can receive Communion twice in one day. We had Communion at the American Mass and then at Father Halley's Mass that day.

When we got back down to the bottom of the mountain, we walked through the vineyards to Vicka's house. Vicka, pronounced "Vishka," is one of the young women visionaries then in their twenties. She and Ivan and Marija, as I noted, still have daily apparitions to date. ABC Television Network had a special on the Apparitions of The Blessed Virgin Mary in 2012 and the interviewer went to Medjugorje to film an interview with Vicka. We watched her in that special as she went through the crowd touching and blessing people and in her one on one interview with the reporter.

In 2012, Vicka was given the gift of healing. But on our trip in 1988, we learned from Father Halley that the Blessed Mother had asked Vicka to suffer for the conversion of the world and for sinners. As a result, she developed a benign brain tumor that caused her extraordinary painful headaches. She suffered for two years. The tumor disappeared a few months before we arrived. Vicka was so open and friendly and smiled all the time unlike Ivan who was quieter and shy.

Both Vicka and Ivan spoke through interpreters. Years later they both spoke English as did Marija. Vicka too spoke of the early years of the apparitions, the efforts of the Communist government to thwart them, Father Jozo's efforts to protect them and of the separate messages from Our Lady for individuals, families, the parish, non-believers and the world. Vicka also told us that when people look up at the cross on Mt. Krizevak, they often see images of the Blessed Mother and the Lamb representing Jesus.

After that my mother did see the image of the Blessed Mother while looking up at Mt. Krizevak, and she saw the image of Our Lord when she looked at the round, glass container holding a large Communion host placed in the middle of what is called the Monstrance (usually a gold stand with a large round ornament on the stand with the Communion host in a round glass container in the middle of the round ornamental piece). When she arrived back in Omaha, mother went up to Father Mel Merwald at St. Margaret Mary's Church and became a Eucharistic Minister (one who gives out Communion at Mass along with the priest). My mother gave out Communion and voted in the May Democratic primary elections a few days before she died seven years ago.

For the rest of the two weeks, we kept the same schedule of breakfast with our hosts, getting to St. James church early for the two rosaries and the American Mass which started at 10:00 a.m. and ended at noon, lunch, events and private prayer. Next we arrived early at 3:30 p.m. at the church for seats to attend the 4:30 p.m.to 6:30 p.m. service of two rosaries, the Blessed Mother's apparition to Ivan followed by the International Mass. It was a prayer routine we cherished. We were praying with Our Lady who was present there.

We got back to Rosa and George's each evening for dinner and visiting with them and each other and took showers with cold water (the houses did not have hot water) and got in bed by 9:30.p.m. One evening all of Rosa and George's children, their spouses and children came to visit.(See a picture of them at the end of the book. I hope it uploaded.) It was a delightful evening. Either their son or their son-in-law was a poet and gave me a book of his poems in Croatian.

One morning, Mary Ann, the mother of Benjamin and Juliette, told us that Benjamin had heard the voice of the Blessed Mother earlier at night. The Blessed Mother spoke to him: "Benjamin, Benjamin, help bring the young people to me." We were excited for him and asked him if she told him how he was to do that. He answered: "No, she didn't tell me." Time would tell.

The last day in Medjugorje, the entire group took the bus back to Dubrovnik. We stayed overnight. Most of our group was flying out the next afternoon. There were the six of us who were flying out that same evening, my mother and me included. In the morning, Father Halley took all of us to the church of St. Blaise. St. Blaise is the saint known for healing the throat and illnesses of the throat. His feast day is celebrated with the priest holding two blessed crossed candles at the throat of each person in line and saying a blessing. Father Halley said Mass for us in the church or basilica named after St. Blaise. Mary Ann and Marie, who had beautiful voices, sang the songs for Mass. There was a relic of Saint Blaise in a glass case there. It was part of his leg and it had miraculously turned to gold.

Father had arranged for us who remained in Dubrovnik to go to the Franciscan Monastery to pray in the chapel, or small room within the church. A nun speaking Croatian indicated to us that the chapel was being closed. We held up our rosaries to let her know that we were praying, but she thought our gesture meant that we wanted rosaries. She motioned to us with her hand to go in a room next to the altar. It was the room where the priest dressed in his vestments or clothes for Mass. The room is called the Sacristy. The nun opened a two door cupboard with over a hundred rosaries hanging on hooks.

She took a few of the rosaries in her hands and offered them to us and pointed to all the rosaries on the cupboard doors, gesturing that we should take some. She said "Medjugorje". We interpreted that to mean the rosaries were blessed in Medjugorje. I saw some rosaries that were midnight blue with gold on the beads like little blue globes of the world with the continents being the gold. I bought four rosaries, one for each of my twin daughters Mary Kay and Elizabeth and one for my niece Allie. I didn't know who the fourth rosary was for but I would soon learn. Marie bought sixteen of the same rosaries to give to her children and grandchildren.

We left the church to go to the boat for our afternoon cruise that Father Halley had arranged for us. On the boat we met a family from California. We told them that we had just come from Medjugorje. They wanted to hear all about our trip there. We told them the story about the Franciscan Monastery and the chapel, about the nun, and about the cupboard with all the rosaries. Marie and I took out the rosaries we bought there and showed them to the family. All of a sudden we both exclaimed: "The chains have turned to gold!"

We heard that having the chains of your rosary turn to gold was one of the little miracles Our Lady gives, along with the Miracle of the Sun, to reward pilgrims for coming to be with her in Medjugorje.

We caught our plane that night. We flew into the airport at Frankfort, Germany. When we got to the terminal, we spotted a sister from Mother Teresa of Calcutta's order of sisters. Mother and I went immediately over to visit her. Mother told her that she had met Mother Teresa once in Omaha when Mother Teresa was given the Humanitarian of the Year Award by Boys Town.

(Boys Town originally was founded by Father Flanagan for homeless boys but later it became Boys and Girls Town because Boys Town is a legal town under the laws of the State of Nebraska and it cannot discriminate against girls. The movie 'Boys Town' was about the early days when Father Flanagan founded his first home for boys. The actor Mickey Rooney played one of the boys. Father Flannigan is up for beatification, a step toward being declared a saint by the Catholic Church.)

We told sister that Mother Teresa stayed with the Poor Clare Sisters of Omaha in their cloistered convent. Sister Mary Clare, the Abbess there, called my mother to come over to meet Mother Teresa. Mother Teresa gave my mother her relic of St. Therese the Little Flower of Jesus. During that private visit with my mother, Mother Teresa encouraged her to volunteer at Francis House. My mother recruited our friend Helen to volunteer with her and for years they cooked and served meals for people in need. I helped them but not as frequently as they did.

94

Sundance and Cherokee Moon

(Francis House has always been thought to be named after St. Francis of Assisi who as a wealthy young man gave up his wealth and started an order of priests called the Franciscans, the same order of priests serving in Medjugorje. But Francis House was also named for Frank McGill, a contractor who generously helped fund and build the facility of Francis/Siena House. He is the brother of my friend Patty McGill Smith.)

I told Mother Teresa's sister that we heard that the Communist government was denying a visa for Mother Teresa to visit Medjugorje. Sister confirmed that. I reached into my purse and took out the fourth rosary and asked sister if she was going to see Mother Teresa soon. I told her the story of the four rosaries being blessed by the Blessed Mother and of the chains turning to gold. She told me she would see Mother Teresa the next day and would give the rosary to her and extend our greetings.

The trip on the airplane took over 24 hours each way. When we arrived back in New York, the customs official was not going to let us take our containers with the blessed rocks and earth from Apparition Hill until we explained they were from Medjugorje. She apparently had heard of Medjugorje for she let us take them into the country. When we arrived in Chicago, I got a migraine headache and left the others to find a cup of coffee to stop the headache. I got lost and couldn't even correctly dial the phone to have my mother paged. It took a half hour, but I finally found them. By this time I was thoroughly exhausted and suggested to my mother that we stay overnight in an airport hotel and fly back to Omaha the next day. She agreed.

The next morning, I awoke at 6:00 a.m., and I knew instantly that I had to get paper and pen. I experienced automatic writing. The words just poured from my head to my hand with the pen and onto the paper. I was given three separate messages. The first message was the instruction to develop a phone card that a person could insert into a pay phone and be able to make phone calls without coins. The call would be on the person's next bill.

The second message was to establish a corporation where the employees were the owners, where it provided child and adult day care, a library and a prayer or meditation room and the employees would have time to study and meditate as part of their work, and where the company gave a fixed portion of its profits to charity.

The third message was to establish an international women's prayer group, and I started writing all the names that came into my head starting with Mrs. Anwar Sadat. Needless to say, I was amazed but uncertain how I would accomplish any of these things. I felt a little like Benjamin must have felt when the Blessed Mother asked him to bring the young people to her.

CHAPTER 4: BACK HOME

Later that afternoon, we flew into Omaha. When I got home, I got a call from Helen. She asked me if I would accompany her and her late husband's Syrian Orthodox priest and his wife to Sioux City, Iowa the next day to hear Mrs. Sadat speak. "You won't believe this," I said. Then I told her about the automatic writing and the three messages including the one about the international women's prayer group and that Mrs. Sadat's was the first name that came to me to put on the list of women. I drove up to Sioux City with Helen and Father and his wife, and we checked into our rooms. I brought the royal blue bag I took to Medjugorje. In it were two Icon pictures of Our Lady of Medjugorje and my notes of the three automatic messages.

I brought one of the Icon pictures of Our Lady of Medjugorje to dinner. I wanted to give it to Mrs. Sadat. We sat at round tables. Helen encouraged me to tell Father and his wife about my trip to Medjugorje, and I showed them the picture of the Icon of Our Lady of Medjugorje. I told Father that I brought it for Mrs. Sadat because I had heard that the Blessed Mother had appeared in Cairo, Egypt. These initial apparitions of Mary, the Mother of God, from 1968 to 1971 at the Zeitun District of Cairo, Egypt were seen above a Coptic Christian Church by estimated crowds of between 250 thousand and a million people of all religious beliefs including Muslims. There have been many other apparitions of the Blessed Mother sited in Egypt even up to 2011.

Mrs. Sadat, an advocate for peace in the Middle East, is the wife of Anwar Sadat, President of Egypt from 1970 until his assassination October 6, 1981. In 1973, he led Egypt into war with Israel to win back Egypt's Sinai Peninsula taken by Israel in the Six Day War of 1967. In 1979 at the invitation of U.S. President Jimmy Carter, President Sadat entered into peace negotiations with Israel Prime Minister Menachem Begin resulting in the Egypt-Israel Peace Treaty. Both President Sadat and Prime Minister Begin were awarded the Nobel Peace Prize in late 1979. There was opposition in Egypt to the peace treaty and on October 6, 1981, President Sadat was assassinated. It was thought that he was assassinated because of his efforts for peace.

Sundance and Cherokee Moon

Back in Sioux City, Father asked me for the Icon picture of Our Lady of Medjugorje and said he would write a note to Mrs. Sadat on the back of the picture. He told Mrs. Sadat that this was a gift from me and that I had obtained the picture in Medjugorje, Yugoslavia where I had just returned from where the Blessed Mother of Jesus has been appearing since 1981. He wrote that I was aware of the apparitions of the Blessed Mother in Cairo in 1968 through 1971. Then Father got up from his chair and went up to Mrs. Sadat's table and gave her the picture. She told him to thank me.

Mrs. Sadat's speech that night was wonderful and all about efforts to bring about peace in the Middle East just as her husband and Prime Minister Begin of Israel had done in 1979. After her speech, Mrs. Sadat asked for questions from the audience. I waited until the last person asked a question, and I went up to the microphone and asked Mrs. Sadat if she would lead us in a prayer for peace in the Middle East. She spoke the most beautiful prayer. Afterward, everyone applauded her. Later we visited her in the hotel lobby. She was staying there too. Father introduced me to her as the woman who gave her the Icon of the Blessed Mother of Medjugorje. Mrs. Sadat told me: "The people of Egypt love the Blessed Mother."

When I got back home, I wrote my friend Nick Johnson, professor of communication law at the University of Iowa in Iowa, City, Iowa. Nick is a former commissioner of the F.C.C. (Federal Communications Commission) in Washington, D.C. appointed by President Lyndon Johnson. I had met Nick when I worked for the Robert F. Kennedy Memorial. The Memorial sponsored a group called the Citizens Communications Corps and Nick was very close to that group.

I wrote to Nick about my three automatic writing messages. He researched the phone card and found that it was in use in New Zealand. I didn't understand why I was given this message. Was I to do something with it? Soon, it would become impossible for me to do anything with it. I realized years later that the phone card message was verification that my automatic messages were real. It also supported the theories of the great psychiatrist Carl Jung and others including that great international spiritual leader Deepak Chopra that there exists a collective consciousness where ideas originate and come directly from God.

The Sunday after we returned from Medjugorje, my mother, my daughter Elizabeth and I drove up to Minneapolis to share our experiences with my baby sister Alice and her husband Jim. We were in Iowa and my mother raised her voice: "Mary Kay, I can see the Miracle of the Sun!" I looked and I could see it too. My daughter Elizabeth was napping in the back seat and she raised her head and said: "Mother, it will be with us all the way to Minneapolis!" I don't know how Elizabeth knew this, but it was true, the Miracle of the Sun followed us all the way up. This was the first time we saw the Miracle of the Sun in America. It was Elizabeth, during her first and only visit to St. Margaret Mary's Church in Omaha attending Father Whelan's Mass and healing service, along with my mother, Helen and me heard the loud voice speak to us: "Father Whelan is a beacon and a light to heal the nation and you are to bear witness to this." My sister Alice was excited about our trip and shared our wonder over our experiences. She loved the religious gifts we brought back for her and her family.

Back home, I arranged for an appearance before the Omaha City Council to report on our trip about getting the Key to the City for the Blessed Mother from Mayor Calinger and all the miracles we witnessed. Our presentation was by Father Halley, S.J., Mary Ann, Marie, my mother and me. We were well received.

We shared the excitement and gifts with the rest of our family and friends and took religious articles blessed by Our Lady of Medjugorje to our friends the Poor Clare Sisters who had prayed for Crystal and her case and for our family since my grandparents Pat and Bess Phelan were patrons of the order and brought them food for years.

I brought a crucifix for my friend Rich Keppen who started a program to help homeless men obtain work and housing called Anthony House. He called me later and told me that the corpus, the body of Jesus, kept changing colors from brown to green. I couldn't explain this but said that green was the color of hope and spring and of money.

During the month after our return, I got the message: "Take rosaries to the poor." I bought rosaries and prayer cards showing people how to pray the rosary and got them blessed by Father Robert Shanahan, S.J., my sister's and my mother's friend. I took them to Hill Top Housing, at 24th and Lake Street, a low rent project of the Omaha Housing Authority. I found a spot and knelt down and prayed the rosary while watching the Miracle of the Sun. I gave the rosaries to the children as they came home after school. The next day, I was told to bring the dogs to pray with me. I brought T-Bear and Hershey, my girls' dogs, to pray with me. When the children came to pet the dogs, I gave them rosaries and prayer cards.

Sundance and Cherokee Moon

The third day I brought the dogs and a big box of blessed rosaries and prayer cards and after praying during the Miracle of the Sun, I sat on a porch and children came up to me to get rosaries with their mothers standing in the doorways urging them on. The last rosary was mine blessed by the Blessed Mother in Medjugorje and it was hanging around my neck and a young man came up to me as I was leaving and said: "Can I have one?"

"You must be special," I said and I explained to him that I was giving him my rosary as I was taking it from my neck and that my rosary came from a village overseas where the Blessed Mother appears and she blessed my rosary. The boy smiled and went happily away. I knew that anyone knowing me who hadn't gone to Medjugorje would think I was crazy, but being obedient to my inner voice, Jesus, I did as I was told. And the joy on the faces of these children and their mothers was my reward.

A while after that, Mary Clarkson, who also went to Creighton University Law School but a year ahead of me, entered into a settlement with HUD whom she had sued to eliminate the crime infested projects and substitute scattered site housing in single family homes, apartments and town houses instead. I hoped that the prayers of the children and their mothers helped achieve that settlement.

100

BOOK II: CHEROKEE STATE MENTAL HOSPITAL, IOWA

CHAPTER 5: THE ROAD TO CHEROKEE

As I explained earlier, from September 1988, the month before we went to Medjugorje, I was receiving inner locutions or inner speakings from the Lord confirmed by Father Bill Whelan. In November, I was planning to take a trip to Topeka, KS to attend the trial of a civil rights lawyer I knew brought against him by the Kansas Attorney General who denied that the civil rights attorney had gotten a settlement in cash in a sexual harassment case against the Attorney General. Unbeknown to the Attorney General, the civil rights attorney had photocopied each one of the $100.00 bills that the Attorney General had paid. Obviously the money was out of his pocket and not taxpayer funded.

Fred Thompson was representing the civil rights attorney. I knew of Fred Thompson from his role as attorney for Marie Ragghianti, a Tennessee Parole Board member who blew the whistle on the pay-for-parole scandal between the Governor and the board members. In order to get a parole, kickbacks had to be paid to the Governor and the Parole Board members. As a result of Marie's and Fred's efforts the Governor and the other Parole Board members went to prison.

I had seen the movie about Marie's and Fred's efforts called *Marie: A True Story* and Fred Thompson played himself in the movie, thus starting a long movie career. He later became U.S. Senator Fred Thompson from Tennessee and a Republican Presidential candidate Fred Thompson.

(The excellent civil rights attorney was named Fred Phelps from Topeka. He was also a pastor. Years later he and his children would become hated people because they turned virulent anti-gay people. They demonstrated at funerals for veterans. Ironically just before he died Fred Phelps befriended a gay group located near the church and his family denounced him.) I personally met Fred Phelps in his good days champion the civil rights of individuals.

A few days before I left, I had gotten the inner message to take the dogs to the lake and pray. So, I took them to the dam site on north 72nd Street where my girls Mary Kay and Elizabeth along with the dogs and me had gone frequently to picnic and walk around the lake.

There were two other reasons to take this trip to Topeka. One was that I could see my friend Dave Holloway at the Veterans Administration Hospital there in Topeka where he was being treated for mental illness, and lastly to get away for a little while since some family members were getting nervous about my inner speakings.

Earlier in the day, I was visiting with my friend and first client Lucy Nelson at a South Omaha restaurant. Her mother and others were there with her. During the conversation, Lucy talked about the pastor at St. Adelbert's parish. The women in the parish were upset because he started swearing at all of them. I got the message that his behavior was because he was stroke prone. I told them I would try to talk to Father. I prayed over what I would say to him.

Father graciously let me into the rectory. I explained that I had just been to Medjugorje in Yugoslavia where the Blessed Mother has been appearing to six young people. I offered him a couple of the blessed stones from Medjugorje but he put his hand up to stop me. I told him that I had been getting messages and that one of the messages was that he should see a neurologist. He immediately stood up and literally forced me out of the rectory and slammed the door behind me.

I was traveling north on 24th Street now and neared St. Ann's Church and got a message to stop there. I rang the bell at the rectory and young Father Kevin Kraft answered the door. I told him that I had just been on a pilgrimage to Medjugorje and that I had brought back some of the blessed stones from Apparition Hill blessed there by the Blessed Mother. Father graciously took the stones and thanked me.

The next parish I came upon and was told to stop at was St. Peter's Parish where I had gone to grade school. The pastor opened the door and I introduced myself and told him that I had gone to grade school there. He directed me into his office. I told him that I had just returned from a pilgrimage to Medjugorje where the Blessed Mother has been appearing to six young people. I took out a few of the small stones and while handing them to him told him that the Blessed Mother had blessed these stones.

Sundance and Cherokee Moon

Father became very angry and threw the stones into his ash tray. Then, he came around his desk and grabbed my hand and literally dragged me into the church and up to the altar and made me kneel in front of a statue of Our Lady of Fatima. He removed one of the statue's hands and put it in mine and told me there was only one apparition and that was in Fatima. He ordered me to pray to Our Lady of Fatima. I prayed to her all right. I prayed for this priest.

A few years later I was able to find out what happened to these three priests. The pastor at St. Adelbert's was in a nursing home after a massive stroke. Father Kevin Kraft died of cancer. And the pastor at St. Peter's had a breakdown and was holed up in the church with guns. There was a long standoff and eventually someone got him to surrender. He had to take a disability retirement. Luckily there was no loss of life. Sometime later when I was telling Father Bill about these incidents, he told me that there had been robberies at St. Peters and that Father had guns to protect the church. It was Father Bill who told me the priest retired on disability.

Back to my trip, I no sooner got back on the highway when I heard on the news that the trial had ended. So, I decided I would make a trip to Des Moines, Iowa, to see my old boss former U.S. Senator from Iowa Harold E. Hughes. I wanted to talk to the Senator about my inner locutions because when I worked for him in his U.S. Senate office in Washington, D.C., the United States Capitol, during the time that he was running for U.S. President, he let it be publicly known that God spoke to him.

As I proceeded driving toward Des Moines, I saw a sign on the road with the words "Underwood, Iowa" on it. All of a sudden I experienced a crippling premonition of my own death. I was so panic stricken that I turned off the highway into a parking lot of a restaurant surrounded by woods. I didn't know if there was something mechanically wrong with the car, if someone had tampered with it, or if I was going to be in a fatal accident, but I was visibly shaken and filled with fear.

I immediately got into my purse and took out the little bottle of oil blessed by Father Bill and my rosary and I got out of the car. I made little signs of the cross with the oil on each of the four doors, the rear bumper and the hood of the car by the front wind shield. Then I opened the hood and opened all four car doors and let the dogs out to run in the far side of the woods. I walked past the front of the restaurant into the near side of the woods. The dogs on the far side were a distance away. I had my rosary with me and I prayed all three sets of mysteries, the Joyful, the Sorrowful, and the Glorious, all fifteen decades of the rosary, five decades for each mystery. It took over an hour.

Then, I silently asked God: "If the car is safe to drive, tell the dogs to get into the car." I could see the dogs in the far distance. Suddenly they both ran back behind the restaurant, across the parking lot and climbed into the car and sat upright facing front. For years I thought that either God had spoken to them or they had extrasensory perception or ESP.

Recently I was reading Deepak Chopra's book *The Spontaneous Fulfillment of Desire: Harnessing the Infinite Power of Coincidence.* Dr. Chopra explains phenomena such as I experienced with my children's dogs as an example of synchronicity which he defines as non-local communication. He says there have been studies on humans and animals that experience this synchronicity. He gave the example of the dog of an owner always waiting at the door just when the owner is to arrive even though the owner arrives at different times each night.

I closed the four car doors and got into the driver's seat and started the car still amazed at the dogs' behavior. After driving about an hour I was feeling tired so I pulled off the highway when I saw a park on the left side of the highway. I pulled into the parking lot with the car facing the sun, parked and let the dogs out to run. I had the radio on and fell asleep.

All of a sudden I woke up and when I looked out the front window, I saw a vision above the car, a life size vision of Jesus on the Cross, the Blessed Mother facing him and then when I turned, I saw St. Therese, the Little Flower of Jesus on the left side of Jesus facing me. I looked at her and said out loud: "What are you doing here?" Internally I said: "What are you doing in this biblical scene?" Usually when you see this scene, you see the apostle John. Instead I saw this beautiful scene with St. Therese, Our Lord and the Blessed Mother.

I had always been devoted to St. Therese of Liseaux, France. My parents Jim and Betty Green fostered this devotion. St. Therese's parents were so devoted to the Blessed Mother that they gave all their children the first name of Marie even the boys. My parents gave all six of us girls the first name of Mary following the devotion to the Blessed Mother fostered by St. Therese's parents. My two brothers were not named Mary.

104

Sundance and Cherokee Moon

When my dad was John F. Kennedy's working Nebraska co-chairman for his Presidential campaign in Nebraska, Senator and then President Kennedy was always amazed that our parents named all six of their girls "Mary." President Kennedy wrote a letter to our dad and at the end, he wrote: "And how are all the Marys?" One of my sisters has that framed letter hanging in her home.

I got to meet President Kennedy again when he was in the White House after his election when I was working for the summer in Washington, D.C. My dad had told me to contact the President's secretary Evelyn Lincoln from Nebraska. She gave me a tour of the President's suite of offices and stood with her back to his office. I was facing his door. She told me that she couldn't show me his office because he was in there.

All of a sudden the door opened and the President walked out. Mrs. Lincoln could tell by the surprised expression on my face that he was behind her. She turned and introduced me to him as Jim Green's daughter from Nebraska. The President said to me: "I have met you before haven't I? You are one of the Marys." "Yes," I answered. "It is nice to see you again Mary." I was so thrilled at getting to see the President in the White House that I called my parents and all my relatives collect and I never wore that dress again. I still have it in my convent trunk. It is stainless.

I was so devoted to St. Therese that when I was sexually abused in a downtown movie theater at age ten by a man, I didn't tell anyone, not my parents, my grandparents or my siblings, my cousins or my friends. The only person I told was St. Therese. I went to the back of our church, St. Peter's in Omaha, and told St. Therese, at her statue, all about my paralyzing abuse. This was a secret I kept until I was fifty years old. Like most victims of abuse, I thought there was something wrong with me that this man would abuse me.

My twin daughters Mary Kay and Elizabeth Marie were also named after the Blessed Mother Mary and they were born on October 1st, the feast day of St. Therese. I kept wondering if she appeared to me because of my girls, was she protecting my girls. This might be, but a few years later I saw a series about her life on EWTN, Mother Angelica's Eternal Word Television Network.

I learned that St. Therese's father spent years in a mental hospital while she was in the convent. I had earlier read a biography about her that indicated that she suffered from neurasthenia which was defined as having one's emotions create physical illnesses. St. Therese asked Our Lord to let her share in his suffering and it is clear that she suffered and willingly suffered to save souls. She had Tuberculosis and she died from the disease. Anyway, I call her the saint for people with mental and emotional illness, and I pray to her for people I love who suffer emotional and mental illness including myself.

In 2000, Pope John Paul II named St. Therese the saint for the Second Millennium and he had St. Therese's relics and a photo exhibition of her life as a girl and in the convent sent around the world. I saw an article in *Newsweek Magazine* about this and the article listed the places in America where the relics and exhibition would be at. One of the places was Sioux City, Iowa at the Carmelite Convent there. St. Therese was a Carmelite nun. Again, I took my mother with me as I had taken her to Medjugorje. We waited in line for several hours with over 6,000 people that day for our turn to touch the reliquary, a beautiful, large wooden box containing her relics.

We were all given laminated prayer cards with St. Therese's picture on them, and we were told to touch these cards to the reliquary and they would become relics themselves. We had enough cards for our entire family, especially my sister Therese who was named after St. Therese. Therese and her husband Paul were living in Kansas City at the time. I went down to visit them and I told them all about the trip or pilgrimage and that we got blessed photo prayer cards for them. My sister was so excited to learn that I brought her one, that she got up and took the card out of my hand before I could give it to her. She was thrilled with her relic.

After I returned to Omaha with my mother from Sioux City, Iowa, I called the Carmelite convent to thank the sisters for hosting the exhibit of St. Therese's life and the reliquary with her relics. I told the sister on the phone about my vision in Iowa back in 1988 of Jesus on the cross, the Blessed Mother facing him and of St. Therese facing me. Sister said I was very blessed to have seen that vision. Before I hung up, I asked sister what her name was. She replied: "I am Mother Therese." She bore St. Therese's name.

Back at the park in Iowa, November, 1988, an announcement came over the radio that Presidential candidate Michael Dukakis was flying into Des Moines in the early hours of the morning on his way back to Massachusetts to vote for himself as President. I called to the dogs and we left the park. A sign over the park exit read "Vision Park." Three times while I was driving to Des Moines, Hershey got into my lap and forced me to get off the highway. Each time a semi-truck sped by shaking the car.

Each truck had the same sign "England" on the sides and back. An hour later I was in Des Moines at the Michael Dukakis headquarters. I asked for my friend and former Harold E. Hughes co-worker Bonnie Campbell. I knew she was working on Dukakis's campaign. She wasn't there at the time but someone gave me a phone number to get in touch with Senator Hughes. I called and he told me to come over to his office in the morning.

Senator Hughes was waiting for me in his office at the alcoholic treatment center he owned. (He owned another center in Arizona.) I visited with him about my trip to Medjugorje and gave him two books about the apparitions there. I shared with him that I was having inner speakings and that my spiritual advisor told me they were from the Lord. Senator Hughes had admitted to the media in 1971 when he was running for President of the United States that God spoke to him.

I relayed to him about the three incidents with the England trucks and asked him what they meant. He said he didn't know. He walked me out the door to the car where the dogs were waiting for me and said: "Where are you going now?" "I am going up to Minnesota to visit my sister." "You know that your family is going to try to have you committed." I told him: "Yes, I know." "Protect yourself," he replied.

I got in the car and drove north toward Minneapolis. I immediately began praying for England. We always prayed for peace in Northern Ireland at our weekly healing Masses with Father Bill, but we never specifically prayed for England. After the incidents with the three England trucks, I started praying for England.

Ten years later on April 10, 1998, the Good Friday Peace Accord was signed between the Catholics and Protestants of Northern Ireland. As I previously told you, Northern Ireland is considered an English country of the United Kingdom which consists of England, Wales and Scotland. The accord was signed by Catholic leader John Hume and Protestant Northern Ireland Prime Minister David Trimble. President Bill Clinton had a role in achieving the accord by appointing former U.S. Senator George Mitchell as negotiator with the warring factions in Northern Ireland. The President was supported in these efforts by British Prime Minister Tony Blair. That same year, John Hume and David Trimble were awarded the Nobel Peace Prize for their efforts in achieving peace in Northern Ireland. It didn't hurt that peace in Northern Ireland was prayed for all those years by Irish men and women all over the world and I assume English men and women.

I decided to take the back roads to Minneapolis rather than the Interstate so that I could avoid the big trucks. I went through a small Iowa town called Lakeview. It was later in the afternoon, and the dogs and I hadn't eaten. I stopped at a burger drive-through restaurant and bought hamburgers for me and the dogs. I spotted an old fashioned hotel and took a room. We ate our hamburgers and then the panic over the premonition took over me again. I began praying the rosary again while begging God to let me live. I told him that my teenage daughters were not ready to be on their own. Surely, I asked: "Don't you have more work for me to do?" I remembered the first words the Lord had spoken internally to me: "I have work for you to do and all that I ask is that you be celibate unless you marry."

Remember, I told you that I was thrilled then but not surprised when I experienced that first inner speaking from the Lord. I say this because of the gift I gave to God of the rest of my life when I was ill in 1982 and thought I was dying. And I was not surprised by this inner speaking from the Lord because of the messages I was receiving from him through Father Bill. Here I was six years later in a motel in Lakeview, Iowa, begging God for more time. I prayed for a long time and then lay down. The dogs came and sandwiched me between them and the warmth of their bodies comforted me. I fell into a deep sleep.

In the morning, I got dressed and led the dogs outdoors and into the back seat of the car. We drove for a little while and I spotted a cemetery. I drove in, parked and let the dogs run for awhile. I spotted a ten foot tall crucifix in the middle of the cemetery and walked over and started to pray. It was cold that day and the sky was grey and cloudy. I prayed for God's protection.

After a while I called to the dogs but they just kept playing. I was anxious to get on the road. When they still wouldn't come, I got into the car and started the motor. They still didn't come so I slowly drove toward the exit. All of a sudden they started to run after the car. I stopped and let them in and proceeded down the road. I should have heeded their reluctance to leave.

Sundance and Cherokee Moon

I came to an intersection and slowly crossed the road. I could not really see well because the dogs' breathing steamed up the windows. It was a new car lent to me and I couldn't find the defrost knob. The dogs started barking furiously and Hershey tried to get on my lap again. I spoke out loud: "Who listens to dogs any how?" This would be my second mistake of the day—not listening to the dogs.

Any dog owner could have told me to listen to my children's dogs. The impact was sudden. I had only been going about five miles per hour. I checked the dogs and they were not injured. I wasn't injured. I got out of the car and saw that I had run into the side of a big, white utility truck. I hadn't heard it coming because the dogs were barking so loud and I could not see it because the windows kept fogging up. The truck must have been traveling fast because I did not see it coming.

I looked at the front of the car and the front of the car had been smashed like a tin can up to the place where I had anointed the car with the blessed oil from Father Bill. I must have been in shock because I started speaking rapidly. I tried to slow down my speech but I couldn't. We were stopped by open fields, and I used my hand and started blessing the fields. One of the deputies who came on the scene asked me what I was doing, and I replied "I am blessing the farmer's field."

Father Bill always taught us to bless people and things. I still bless people and things silently in my mind and I say: "Dear God, please bless so and so," but I no longer use my hands. I had my keys in my hand and took the little round ten bead rosary key from the chain and gave it to the deputy. I told him that this key was blessed by the Blessed Mother in Medjugorje, Yugoslavia, and that's why we weren't injured. He smiled and took the key.

A tow truck came and towed the car to a gas station back in Lakeview. The officer drove me and the dogs to a motel in the city. I got a room for the three of us and as soon as we were in the room I called my friend Mary Cornett in Omaha. I told her about the accident and asked her to get a hold of my friend Rich Keppen and ask him to come pick us up in Lakeview. I gave her his phone number. I tried to call her back but I kept dialing the wrong number. I couldn't remember her phone number. This was as frustrating as my experience with the phone in the Chicago airport on the way back from Medjugorje. Suddenly I became tired so I decided to take a nap until Rich got there. The dogs again sandwiched me in between them. It must have been several hours until I heard a knock at the door.

My mother and my sister Liz came to get me. Liz was driving her husband's new car and said we couldn't take the dogs with us. They wanted me to abandon my girls' dogs in Lakeview. There was no way that I would do that. They went across the parking lot to get coffee, and I locked the door behind them as they left. I looked in the phone book for the number of a veterinarian's office. I called the only one. I was informed that they only took dogs for boarding thirty pounds or less. I was told there was a vet thirty minutes away that took bigger dogs and I was given the name and phone number of a Vietnam War veteran I could call to drive me to place the dogs.

When Mark, the Vietnam War vet arrived, I told my mother and my sister that I was taking the dogs to board them and that I would be right back. But when I got in the car with the dogs, I changed my mind and told Mark I would pay him to take me to Akron, Iowa near Sioux City to my friends where I could leave the dogs. My friends Tom and Betty Everingham were relatives of my long time friend Joanie Noonan Liddell and her sister Terry Noonan Liddell. Both Joanie and Terry married cousins named Dave. Betty Noonan Everingham was their older sister.

I met Joanie first, in 1965, when we were both part of the first anti-poverty program in Omaha. The program was sponsored by the Omaha Catholic Archdiocese. Joanie had just graduated from Duchene Women's College of the Sacred Heart in Omaha and I had graduated from Creighton University there, a Jesuit university. Eighteen of us young women and young men moved into the near north side, the segregated black community in Omaha which was called the "ghetto" by many in the city. Open housing wasn't the law in Omaha until 1972 when the Omaha City Council passed an Open Housing Ordinance. The ordinance was sponsored by two Catholic City Council members Monte Taylor, a Republican and John Miller, a Democrat. Both men were trial lawyers.

We organized the neighbors and taught them community action principals to get the area more services from the city. We also started a girls club. The community already had the Boys Club of America chapter, but there was nothing for girls. Our sponsors were two Catholic priests Father James Stewart and Father Jerry Burbach. They were followers of the great community organizer from Chicago Saul Alinsky. (President Barack

110

Sundance and Cherokee Moon

Obama was influenced by Alinsky when he was a community organizer in Chicago.) Many years later both priests left the priesthood and married.

I left the program early when I got a job with Deputy Attorney General John Doar at the U.S. Department of Justice Civil Rights Division in Washington, D.C. as a docket room clerk in the Civil Rights Division. Mr. Doar told me that there were no openings yet for me to be an investigator and he asked me to go into the docket room and help him straighten it out. The government Vista anti-poverty volunteers took over the Archdiocese program the next year. Joanie joined the Peace Corps and went to South America.

My girls and I had been up to Tom and Betty's acreage outside of Akron one winter when Joanie was visiting them. Tom and Betty took all of us and their own son Tommy to a neighbor's farm to take horse driven sleigh rides in the snow. This was right after Christmas that year. The summer of 1987, I came up to see Joanie and Tom and Betty when Joanie was visiting with them again. After dinner Joanie and I sat outside on the deck. The sky was midnight blue filled with bright stars.

We could see red lights up in the distant sky and speculated they could be outer space vehicles or spy planes and laughed. The night was so beautiful and we talked a long time catching up on each other's lives. It had been five years since Joanie's Dave had committed suicide in despair of ever getting well. He suffered from rapid cycling bi-polar illness with multiple extreme ups and downs several times a day. Dave was one of my three male friends who died in the same month in 1982 and my daughter Elizabeth's godfather. Joanie was her godmother.

That night in 1988, Mark, the Vietnam Veteran visited with Tom and Betty and left to go back to Lakeview. I visited with Tom and Betty while Tom fixed dinner. I told them all about the pilgrimage that my mother and I had just taken to Medjugorje and all the miracles we saw there. I told them all about visiting with Senator Hughes in Des Moines and that I had gotten in a car accident near Lakeview on my way to Minneapolis to visit my sister Alice and her husband Jim. I didn't tell them about the fact that my mother and my sister Liz had come up to Lakeview to take me home and that they wanted me to abandon my daughters' dogs. I did tell them about the spiritual experiences I was having and asked Betty if she would help me see a Catholic psychiatrist so I could verify that my experiences were real. Betty is a nurse.

111

We were sitting around the table talking when the phone rang. All Betty said was "yes," and she hung the phone up. We went on talking. About an hour later there was a knock on the door. A sheriff's deputy was at the door. I immediately rushed downstairs. I knew why he was there.

I got into my purse and took out my razor and my nail clippers to go back upstairs just at Betty came down. I told her that Senator Hughes told me that my family would try to commit me because of my spiritual experiences and to protect myself. I told her about my mother and my sister coming to take me back to Omaha and demanding that I abandon the dogs. She said if I had only confided in her she would not have told them I was there. She begged me to come up with her because two deputies had grabbed Tom and forced him face down on the floor when he was trying to protect me.

I went up ahead of her and told the deputies that I was Mary Kay Green. They told me that they had a court order to take me. I was supernaturally calm. When they realized how calm I was, they didn't handcuff me. They asked me to sit in the front seat. A female officer sat in the back with the other deputy. They didn't tell me where they were taking me and I didn't ask. We drove what seemed like hours, and then as the car turned into a private road, the headlights shined on a sign: "Cherokee State Mental Hospital." Just like the prophecy I had gotten from Father Bill warning me that all the people in my civil rights trial against the city last summer would turn against me, God warned me again, this time through Senator Hughes who told me: "Your family is going to try to have you committed. Protect yourself." I was emotionally prepared.

CHAPTER 6, CHEROKEE I, 1988

It was three a.m. in the morning when an Indian psychiatrist on call at Cherokee State Mental Hospital in Cherokee, Iowa, finished interviewing me. I explained to him that I had just been on a pilgrimage to Medjugorje, Yugoslavia, with a group of people from Omaha, where the Blessed Mother has been appearing to six young people called visionaries since 1981. I told him that we had witnessed miracles such as our rosary chains turning to gold and seeing the Miracle of the Sun. He asked me a number of questions assessing my touch with reality, and finally said: "I find nothing wrong with you. You are free to go."

"Free to go?" I thought. I was pretty tired at this point. "I am in the middle of no where miles away from my friends Tom and Betty Everingham, and no offer of a ride back to my friends." It was the middle of the night, now 4 a.m., and I didn't think I should call Tom and Betty at this hour. I asked the doctor if I could spend the night there and make arrangements to leave in the morning. I was given a bed and I slept in my clothes.

I had a light blue sweater and light blue pleated skirt outfit on, and a wooden rosary from Medjugorje blessed by the Blessed Mother around my neck. Everyone in Medjugorje wore rosaries. It was such a freeing feeling to be able to openly express your faith. While I was growing up in Omaha, there was discrimination against Catholics. The long term superintendent Harry Burke of the Omaha Public Schools refused to hire Catholic teachers. There were no anti-discrimination laws then. This was just one example.

Today Catholics in Middle Eastern Muslim countries are being martyred, and crucified because of their religion, especially in Syria and Iraq by a radical army called ISIS. These men murder Muslims too.

In the morning I was informed by the psychiatrist in charge of the women's unit that my family had gotten a judge to put a hold on me until there could be a hearing. A nurse had told me the doctor wanted to talk to me. This doctor was white. I make a point of this because most of the doctors were of color from various foreign countries. Few doctors go into

113

psychiatry since it is the lowest paying of the medical specialties so doctors from foreign countries can get visas to work in America as needed professionals.

I told the doctor about my car accident with my daughters' dogs in the car with me. And I explained that my mother and sister came to get me but wouldn't let me bring the dogs with me because my sister was driving her husband's new car. I told him how I hired a Vietnam War veteran to drive me and the dogs to my friends outside of Akron, Iowa near Sioux City.

The doctor asked me if I had any history of mental illness. I told him that I suffered deep depression after the deaths of people I love. He asked me if I would agree to be evaluated by two doctors. I agreed.

Later that day, a black psychiatrist from Nigeria and another Indian psychiatrist asked me to follow them to an interview room. They started questioning me. I received an inner message: "Tell them about your spiritual experiences." I immediately shot back internally: "If I do, they will keep me here forever." "Trust me," he said.

I asked the doctors for paper and a pen, and then I wrote all about my pilgrimage to Medjugorje with my mother, about the vision I had two days before with Jesus on the Cross, the Blessed Mother facing him and St. Therese, the Little Flower of Jesus, standing to the left of Our Lord and facing me. I also wrote about seeing the Miracle of the Sun in Medjugorje and here in the United States.

The Indian doctor told me that he is an atheist and said that I was suffering from a form of religious hysteria. He said that the religious beliefs of the people in India were a form of mass hysteria. The Nigerian doctor said to me: "What you write is so lucid." "Of course it was lucid," I said to myself, "I was experiencing extraordinary spiritual experiences." Years later I wrote to Cherokee to get my medical records. I wanted copies of the statement I wrote to the doctors. They were not sent from my file. I assumed that the Nigerian doctor kept them since he thought they were so rational. I will never know if he subsequently learned of the Miracles of Medjugorje from other sources. One thing I did not tell them about was my inner locutions or inner speakings from the Lord.

Well, the doctors decided I was bi-polar. Bi-polar illness is a chronic bio-chemical mood disorder with extremes of highs or mania and lows or depression. In one record, I was also called schizo-affective because of seeing the Miracle of the Sun and rosaries turning gold that I witnessed in Medjugorje and in America and the vision I reported. In another report, a doctor called me a religious fanatic. Schizo-affective disorder is a psychotic disorder where people hear and see things that are not there.

I wasn't sure about being bi-polar, but I surely wasn't Schizo-affective or a fanatic. I did acknowledge that I was vulnerable to deep depression or grief at the death of people I loved and cherished. In 1968 within an eight day period, I lost my hero Robert F. Kennedy to an assassin's bullet and eight days later my father Jim Green died of instant sudden death when three reporters asked him where the Kennedy delegates were going next. He died instantly. My father and I were at the State Democratic Convention June 14, 1968 in Hastings, Nebraska. Dad was working co-chairman of Robert F. Kennedy's Presidential campaign and chairman of the Kennedy delegates to the Chicago Democratic Convention. I was devastated and so was my whole family especially my mother.

In 1982, during the same thirty day period as I reported earlier, three of my close men friends all died. First my friend Dave Liddell, Joanie's Dave, the godfather of my daughter Elizabeth, died from suicide. I attended his funeral in Denver. Next my friend, mentor and former boss attorney Benjamin Wall died from an aneurism. He had survived pancreatic cancer but died years later of an aneurism. Finally on June 12, 1982, my beloved friend and mentor, attorney Arthur O' Leary died of cancer. I had lunch with Art every week for eight years from my first year in law school. I attended Ben's wake and Art's funeral Mass. Working with Ben and Art was like practicing law with my dad who died in 1968, nine years before I would graduate from law school. Ben and Art both died at age fifty-one, the same age as my father.

I was so grief stricken by the deaths of these three men so close to me that I wasn't able to work for six months. My friend Ed Fogarty took over my practice. I needed an anti-depressant and grief counseling but I had lost my health insurance.

Back at Cherokee, when the doctors completed their report, a nurse came and found me and told me that they ordered medication for me. She also gave me a schedule of the films I must watch about the various medications I was to take. I watched the films. In the films, doctors described each medication I was taking, the possible side effects, and

115

stressed the need for compliance, the need to take your medications daily as they were prescribed. It was explained that lack of compliance would result in further episodes of your illnesses.

Voluntary non-compliance would never be a problem for me because Father Bill cautioned us at every healing service that we should never go off medication if we thought we were healed unless a doctor told us to. He stressed that God works through doctors too. Father Bill sent me a note that he was praying for me.

Later that day, the head psychiatrist called me into his office. The reality of my not going home right away had sunk in. I was pretty upset about this. First he wanted to know if that black Nissan at the gas station in Lakeview was my car. He passed that way on his way to work. I told him that it was. "That car was totaled," he said. "I can't believe that you weren't injured in that accident. I am going to order a MRI and a physical examination of you. We have to make sure that you are all right." "There is nothing wrong with me," I said. "We're going to make sure of that," he replied. I was taken to a physician's office for examination and to a mobile trailer for the MRI scan. All the tests showed that I was not injured.

The second thing he wanted to talk to me about was the fact that there would be a mental health commitment hearing in three days. "I want you to know your rights. If the judge commits you, I have to keep you here for ninety days, but if you stay voluntarily, I will have you out of here in two weeks."

I called a lawyer friend of mine to represent me. We had successfully tried a civil rights case together. He and his associate came up the morning of the hearing. We talked it over, and I told him about the ninety days and the two weeks. He was confident that they could win the hearing for me, but I didn't want to take a chance. I remembered the warning that Senator Hughes had given me: "Your family is going to have you committed. Protect yourself." I agreed to stay voluntarily for the two weeks.

My brother Pat, my daughter Elizabeth, my sister Liz and my mother all came up for the hearing. I visited with them for a while after the hearing which I did not attend. Liz didn't say anything, she seemed very upset. Many years later, my daughter Elizabeth told me that Mary Cornett had pressured Liz to have me committed because of the accident. As a young woman, Mary had to commit her grandfather when he was mentally ill.

I had mixed feelings when they left. In fact I was experiencing inconsistent feelings: feelings of glad to see them but also fearing them because they had control over me; feeling protected here temporarily from another accident, yet feeling jailed; and fearful because of the premonition again and wanting to go home.

When it turned dark the second evening I was there, I was overwhelmed with the desire to run to the highway nearby and hitch hike a ride to Omaha, but I feared that I would be picked up by a sheriff's deputy. Surely other people had tried to escape from there and were apprehended. I went behind the building closest to the highway and leaned against the wall sobbing uncontrollably. Eventually I experienced dry tears and resigned, I went back into the building where I was staying.

The first full day I was there, I was approached by three women from our ward. They kindly invited me on a tour of the places where we could go in the buildings. They gave me the unofficial orientation. The first place they took me was down a couple of stairways into the canteen. Inside it was an old fashioned drug store with a counter with a cash register and tables and booths. One of the women bought me a cola. The three could see that I was a little shell shocked at being in the hospital, and they told me stories to make me laugh.

Next they told me about the chapel services. Monday, Wednesday and Friday were the days for Catholic Mass and Tuesday and Thursday were the days for the Protestant services. There was a Catholic priest and a Protestant minister available. I went all five days. The songs were the same for all five services and all the services were attended by both patients and staff. We all prayed together.

After that they told me all about going to the "vampires." Cherokee State Mental Hospital was a series of buildings all connected by underground tunnels. One of these tunnels went underground to the lab where the "vampires" take your blood every morning before breakfast. I was put on lithium and other drugs and they took my blood every morning to make sure there was enough lithium in my blood stream.

Another tunnel went to the recreation building. This building housed the library and the game room. We were only allowed to go there on certain evenings. At one point the rumor went around that there was a rapist in the men's unit. We were all afraid, but I still forced myself to go by myself through the tunnel to the library.

Finally the women told me about movie night and dance night, two separate nights. We would go to an auditorium for these two nights. They also explained that we could see the teenagers on the other side of a grill, but we would be kept separate from them. These three women would be my best friends for my two week stay.

I felt like a normal person with them and in all the places they showed me. I didn't feel normal on the floor. I felt like an inmate. The nurses did not mingle with the patients. They were cloistered behind a wooden barrier. I felt normal every afternoon at the canteen, normal in the chapel before dinner where those of us who chose to go did. I felt normal in the cafeteria where the women cooking and serving for us were so cheerful and caring.

There was one more place where I felt normal and that was outdoors. I was given unlimited opportunity every morning after breakfast, every noon after lunch and late every afternoon to walk freely outdoors. The staff did not know that I wanted to run away that second night I was there. Most of these days, my two weeks there, were sunny. I could see the Miracle of the Sun three times a day at Cherokee that I had first seen in Medjugorje.

Saint Therese, the Little Flower of Jesus, wrote in her autobiography that Jesus is the sun. I first read *The Story of a Soul*, as I noted earlier, when I was a postulant with the Sisters of Mercy at the College of St. Mary in Omaha. I have read St. Therese's book a number of times since then including recently.

When I watched the Miracle of the Sun at Cherokee I was engaged in prayer to Our Lord. Even though I only had one inner speaking or inner locution while at Cherokee, I did a lot of talking to God. I remember saying to him, "Who goes to Medjugorje and ends up thirty days later in a State mental hospital?"

In prayer, I came to the realization that this might have been the reason I was called to Medjugorje. The lore is that Our Lady calls you to go to Medjugorje and she helps you find the money to go. After days of praying and questioning God, I came to the conclusion that he had taken me up on my gift of the rest of my life to him in 1982 when I was so physically ill and in severe grief. I came to the conclusion that this is what he was asking of me—to be mentally ill, to walk in the path of others who suffered mental illness and to be an advocate. I feared that he may be asking me to be institutionalized for the rest of my life but that fear was soon dissipated.

I did get comfort from my three times a day monologues with God. Getting to see the Miracle of the Sun three times a day reassured me that whatever happened, I was in his hands. Seeing the Miracle of the Sun three times a day and my inner locution from him confirmed what Father Bill had told me—that my inner speakings were from the Lord and not from the devil as someone suggested. I remembered my prayer in the cemetery: "Lord, give me a sign." The Miracle of the Sun three times a day for two weeks in Cherokee was my sign. Getting to see the Miracle of the Sun three times a day reassured me that whatever happened, I was in his hands.

Every day at Mass and at the Protestant services a young man came in and said: "I am the devil," and then he would walk out. I had heard of people thinking they were God, and when I was a social worker in the late 1960's with a psychiatric caseload (most of my poor white clients were in treatment) I visited a client in St. Joseph's Mental Hospital. Another patient was walking up and down the halls with her arms extended saying: "I am the angel of God," but I had never met someone before who thought they were the devil. I have met people who acted like the devil, but no one who claimed to be the devil. "The devil" at Cherokee calmed my Catholic fear of the real devil.

The second day, someone came and got me and told me I had a visitor waiting for me in the visiting room. I went there and saw Mark, the Vietnam veteran who rescued me and my girls' dogs. He was with a young woman whose name I can't remember. He said: "I have got to apologize to you. The sheriff came after me when I got back from taking you to your friends, and threatened to arrest me if I didn't tell him where I had taken you. I was so upset that I went out the next day to see Tom and Betty to find out what had happened. They told me that the deputies had taken you to Cherokee Hospital. I said I wanted to visit you. They asked me if I would bring your suitcase with your clothes to you. Are you okay? What's going on?"

I told him all that happened, about the hours driving, of the interview, of not having a ride to go back, of staying overnight, of finding out the next day that a judge had signed an order to keep me here, and that there would be a hearing in two days. "You don't belong in here," he said. I told him that I was having a lawyer I worked with come up and represent me at the hearing. It was time for Mark and his friend to leave. I really didn't want them to go, but I was so grateful they came to visit, and I told them so.

The evening after the hearing, we were allowed to go to the building that housed the library and the recreation room. I went with my new friends. They went to the recreation room and I went to the library. I searched the shelves for something to read and I was drawn to a book written by the famous actress Patty Duke titled *A Brilliant Madness*. It was a book about her life with manic depressive illness, the original name for bi-polar illness.

I was shocked because I had to hold the book high out and up over my right shoulder because I was having trouble focusing my eyes. I had no trouble before I came there so I assumed it was the medications. Patty Duke's experiences with mania were rather spectacular. She had a history of abuse from her handlers when she was a child actress and suffered depression then, but she did get help after being diagnosed and she wrote this book later and she started speaking out all over the country about her mental illness and her recovery. This was in the early 1980's and for a famous actress to expose herself and her illness took a tremendous amount of courage. She gave me the courage to live my life with this illness. I never knew where it would take me or if I would ever live a normal life, but Patty Duke gave me hope.

As I told you, the morning after I arrived at Cherokee, I was on the ward wearing a blue wool pleated skirt and matching sweater and I had a rosary from Medjugorje around my neck. My fellow patients showed me that they thought I was a nun. People kept asking me to pray with them. One woman, a retired teacher, was sitting in one of the chairs at the end of the unit watching "Jeopardy." She had such low self-esteem that she berated herself for watching the show. I told her the show was good for her because it challenged her memory. Then she asked me to pray with her. I was bent down to talk to her so I continued in that position and we prayed together. I was careful not to let the staff know what we were doing so they wouldn't call me a fanatic like that very nice but atheist Indian psychiatrist had.

Beside library and recreation room nights, we had movie nights and dance nights. The first night at dance night a younger man came up to me and

120

asked me to dance. I followed him out to the floor. When he put his arms around me to dance, he asked me to pray for him. I created a special prayer for him. I was no longer wearing my rosary. I had put it in my pocket so I wouldn't be called a religious fanatic but everyone had seen me that first full day with the rosary around my neck like everybody did in Medjugorje. He told me he was a Vietnam Veteran. This was the second Vietnam Veteran in my life in four days. It was appropriate because I had been the military caseworker for Iowa U.S. Senator Harold E. Hughes in Washington, D.C. at the height of the Vietnam War. I was about seven years older than most of those soldiers then and this younger man.

I prayed for all my fellow patients every day at Mass and at the Protestant services and outdoors when I was watching the Miracle of the Sun, I especially prayed for a young woman who was watching Phil Donahue's show *Donahue* at the same time I was. I never told anyone there that I had been on Phil Donahue's show two years earlier with my client Crystal Chambers, now Crystal Chambers Stewart. The show we were watching was about mothers who were responsible for the deaths of their babies.

The young woman was in a rocking chair and was rocking furiously all during the show. I was concerned for her because she seemed so upset. I was picking up on her anxiety and was feeling it myself. I asked her if she was all right. She didn't respond. Later I told my three new friends all about this incident. They told me that some doctor had given this young woman the wrong medicine and she killed her baby. She hadn't been in her right mind.

One night, one of the women patients was screaming all night. It was impossible to sleep not only because of the noise but because I was so concerned about her. There was such anguish in her voice. The next day, the staff surrounded her in a circle and gradually maneuvered her up to the locked ward. My friends always talked about the locked ward as if terrible things happened up there.

One evening after eating dinner, I walked upstairs a different way. I came upon a young woman with her arms around her legs and her head down. I asked her if she was all right. She said: "You can see me? I am a ghost." I touched my hand to her knee and said: "Yes, I can see you. Do you want to go upstairs with me?" "No," she replied, "I want to stay here for a while." I told the nurses upstairs about her and one of them told me they would see to her.

Sundance and Cherokee Moon

I need to tell you about what I call "The Addiction Room." We were all so doped up with these heavy medications and they made us so sleepy, that the nurses threatened to lock our bedroom doors if they caught us in bed. The threat caused constant fear. What they offered us instead was the addiction room. A room with tables and chairs, pots of thick black coffee and tea of the blackest black color both full of caffeine to counter act the side effects of the drugs. The other addiction in that room was cigarettes; so many of the patients smoked for the nicotine that the room was constantly filled with smoke.

I am allergic to cigarette smoke and I couldn't drink the coffee or tea so my counter to the side effects was my constant walking out doors where I would go for exercise and prayer. "Exercise and Prayer," that might make a good title for a book, you know, get healthy and holy in one shot of time.

It wasn't just the drugs that made up sleepy; it was the inability to sleep at night. The old mattresses were covered in old cracked plastic with no mattress covers on top of the plastic. The plastic caused us to sweat all night, and for me, my bed faced a bright light bulb that penetrated my vision and my dreams, so with the sweating and the bright light, I tossed and turned all night. I pray they have bought new mattresses and mattress covers by now. Good sleep is important for everyone but especially for people with mental illness.

Thanksgiving was near and the head psychiatrist told me I could go home to Omaha to see how I could handle it. He said he would call my family. He had to come to me later to tell me that my family was all getting together for Thanksgiving, even my sister from Minnesota and her husband, and that they "couldn't handle it," couldn't handle a visit from me. My reaction was: "I am supposed to be the one who is mentally ill, and they can't handle it." The last big gathering we had in a crisis was when my father died. It was devastating. Years later, I realized that my diagnosis was like a death to them. They got together to mourn me.

The doctor said he would call my fiends Tom and Betty to see if they would have me stay with them for Thanksgiving and the week end. We had a wonderful time together. I dearly loved Tom and Betty. Betty apologized for not telling me that my sister had called to make sure I was there that night the sheriff came. She talked to me again about why I had not told her that my mother and my sister had been there that day to get me. Mark had told them about my mother and my sister being there. I told her that was why I asked her to get me an appointment with a Catholic psychiatrist and I told her about Senator Hughes warning to me that my family was going to have me committed and to protect myself. I told her that I should have confided in her.

When I got out of the hospital, I called Betty in Akron, IA, to thank her. She told me that the doctor had called them after my Thanksgiving stay with them. He asked her how I did. She told him that I was just as normal as the night I was taken to the hospital. She told him that she and Tom could see nothing wrong with me.

Cherokee State Mental Hospital was a series of brick buildings not unlike a college campus. I am not a student of architecture, but inside the red brick buildings with old fashioned green shingles on the roofs, all the units had ceilings that seemed two stories high, and you could tell the buildings were old by the wall paper. Something you would think you would not run into in a state hospital was religious plaques on the walls. There was the famous hands-folded in prayer and a plaque of the Blessed Mother with a halo over her head. I can't remember what other items there were, but they were comforting to me and I assumed to the other patients.

I had a disturbing conversation with one of the three women I hung out with. She told me about our youngest friend. She told me that she had been transferred to the hospital in Iowa City because she was suicidal. It was difficult for me to accept that she was suicidal because she was always the most cheerful of us. I was upset for her because she was suffering and because I didn't get to see her before she left. I have often thought of her and the other fellow patients and wondered how their lives turned out.

In the middle of the second week I was there, the head psychiatrist talked to me about going home. He wanted me to meet with staff to get their consensus. I walked in the room he directed me to and there was the lady from the library, the lady from the canteen and other staff. I realized that they were all part of the treatment and that they were monitoring all my and the other patients behavior. Luckily they all agreed that I was ready to go home.

The doctor gave me permission to call home to see if someone would drive up to pick me up. No one would. I guess they thought this was a permanent placement. I learned from one of my daughters that my sisters were packing up my apartment without asking me, and that not one of them offered a temporary place for me to sleep until I found other housing. They really thought I would be at Cherokee forever. The only reason I was allowed to go home was that I had money in my checking account and the staff bought me a bus ticket to Omaha.

I was asked to attend a group therapy session before I left. This was the first and only therapy session offered at the hospital. The legislature must have cut therapy and therapists from the budget. In the session we were all encouraged to bring up any fears we might have about going home and what we anticipated when we got there. I was not too optimistic.

Before I left the Catholic priest came up to me and told me that he just received a magazine all about Medjugorje. "Mary Kay, I got a magazine in the mail today, and it told all about Medjugorje. Do you want me to tell the doctors?" "No," I replied, "They won't believe me anyway." I had gotten to know Father during my stay and told him all about my pilgrimage to Medjugorje and that the doctors thought I was experiencing religious hysteria.

One of my friends told me that Father had a relative a patient in the hospital. My friend pointed her out to me. She was a young woman. When I got on the bus she was on there too. I sat across from her. She recognized me and said: "Hi." We made a stop on the way and we all got off the bus. She told me that someone was going to pick her up there. We hugged each other and exchanged "Good Lucks." It was comforting to have her on the trip with me. She understood that I was concerned about the rest of the trip and who would come to pick me up.

When I arrived at the bus depot in Omaha, Mary Kay and Elizabeth were there to pick me up. They told me that our friend Mary Cornett wanted me to stay with her. Mary had been a family friend of my parents, and I got close to her when I was an Omaha City Council member. My late friend Mary Cornett was the City Clerk. Mary's daughter Abbie was two years older than Mary Kay and Elizabeth, and the two families socialized a lot. Abbie is like a daughter to me and God gave her and her husband three wonderful daughters, two of them twins my granddaughter Phelan's age. Abbie was prepared for having twins by being friends with my twins. When I was on the City Council for four years, my girls and Abbie would come down to the City Council office after school every Tuesday when we had our meetings.

Sundance and Cherokee Moon

Mary hugged me and showed me that she had made a bed for me on her living room couch. The girls left, and it was late so Mary encouraged me to get some sleep. Her dogs and cat welcomed me too. When I lay down, Red Dog, that was his name, climbed up on top of me. He was heavy, and I was too week to push him off. He slept on top of me all night. Animals know when someone is vulnerable and hurting. He was trying to protect me and comfort me. When Mary got up, Red Dog slid off of me.

I visited with Mary before she went to work. After that my girls picked me up to take me to our town house. My sisters were there moving everything. I walked past the dumpster and saw some of my precious belongings in there. All my Irish records that I bought from the Irish singing groups that toured America and performed in Omaha were in the trash. I would never be able to replace them, and the dumpster was too deep for me to retrieve them. I was exhausted and held back the tears welling up in my eyes. I felt I had lost control of my life. It was more than a thought, it was my new reality. I have subsequently worked with seniors who have had to move into smaller places against their wishes because of their changed circumstances. I could always relate to the pain they were experiencing and shared my story with them.

I had to make plans for a place for me to live. I could no longer economically provide a home for my girls. I could not work because of the heavy medication I was on and because of my vision disturbance. I applied for a one bedroom apartment in my mother's building. At first the owner didn't want to rent to me. He knew who I was and was afraid that I was going to try to organize his tenants. I shared my story with his agent and she told him and he was most compassionate and rented me the apartment. It was in walking distance from my rented town house and still in the Dundee area where I was living and where I had lived for years.

I learned to be more compassionate toward my siblings. Their only experience with disabling mental illness was with our friend Dr. David M. Holloway, M.D. Dave, who grew up in St. Peter's Parish and was a friend of my older brother's, became a fixture with our family, and after medical school and private practice went to Vietnam as a surgeon. The difficult work of trying to patch up so many of our wounded young men and seeing too many of them die had triggered a severe mental illness in him. He was given a psychiatric Air Force disability discharge.

Dave was never able to work again, and he had periodic episodes which usually landed him at the gates of the Strategic Air Base in Bellevue, Nebraska before being hospitalized by his sister. My siblings thought that was my new life. There were times when I wondered about this myself, but time would show otherwise. I talk about Dave later in this book. But I was going to visit Dave at the VA Hospital in Topeka when I went down there for the trial but when the trial was completed, as I learned on the radio, I forgot to call Dave to let him know that I would not be coming down, he called my family frantic.

Years later as I noted earlier, I also learned that it wasn't a family member who urged commitment of me. It was Mary Cornett. Instead of calling my friend Rich Keppen to pick me and the dogs up, she called one of my sisters. As a young woman, Mary had to commit her grandfather. My family members were all acting out of love and fear for me. I understand that now. My brother-in-law had cousins in Iowa who were lawyers, that's how they got the court order so fast.
I can tell you unequivocally today that if I had been among them and one of our other siblings had been in a car accident in another state and had failed to come home with me and I feared for their mental and physical well-being, I would have done something. I am not sure what. As "my old friend" Shirley MacLaine would say, "there are no accidents, no coincidences." I was supposed to be in Cherokee. Ironically, someone did contact Rich Keppen, and he contacted his sister who was in charge over at St. Joseph Mental Hospital in Omaha where she had saved me a bed when they were supposed to bring me home. I guess God wanted me in Cherokee. I would visit St. Joe's down the line.

Now you must understand that I was one of five lawyers among my siblings. No one sat down and said, I think you should apply for Social Security Disability, may I help you. I went down there myself since I had handled Social Security cases before. I gave them all the information about my diagnosis and gave them the contact information for Cherokee State Mental Hospital. Then I got a letter from them. They had assigned a psychologist to interview me and gave me an appointment with her. I knew her from the women's movement although we were not close. She is a good person. She interviewed me and when I feared she was going to find me normal, I told her that God talks to me. I saw the look on her face. I was being honest, but I knew from the way the atheist doctor treated me at Cherokee when I told him and his co-doctor about my vision and the Miracle of the Sun, that this would qualify me. To tell you the truth, there was no way that I could work with all the heavy medication they were giving me and because of my vision problem.

It took me six months for me to receive Social Security payments. This is short compared to what came afterward for applicants. Some people are denied and have to appeal and appeal hearings take two years to get. Until I would receive SSI, I called one of my siblings to see if they could all help me with my rent, and I was made to call each one of them personally for help, my one sibling would not make the calls for me. My status in the family had plummeted. I was no longer the second mother, second oldest sibling. Now I was this mental patient. The checks came like clockwork. I was grateful though humiliated. I fought hard to become independent in my life especially after my girls were born. I found dependency very difficult after becoming successfully independent. I know I am not alone in this feeling.

BOOK III: BACK HOME

CHAPTER 7: 1989

The people at Cherokee made an appointment for me for follow up care at the Douglas County Psychiatric Clinic. The clinic consisted of a large room filled with desks with two chairs per desk, one for the psychiatrist and one for the patient. There was no privacy. One of the doctors I saw there was a woman psychiatrist named Glenda Housel, M.D. She would play a role in my life a few years later. About this time my friend Dave Holloway, M.D., finding out that I had been diagnosed bi-polar sent me a book on bi-polar Illness. Dave was often diagnosed with bi-polar illness at the Topeka Veterans Hospital. The alternate years, the residents diagnosed him with schizophrenia. Each year they changed his medicine. He called himself a Guiney pig.

One time, psychiatrist Kent Meninger, M.D., an adopted son of one the famous Menninger brothers, ordered a combination of drugs that kept Dave normal for two and a half years. They were glory years. I was living in Overland Park, Kansas at the time with Mary Kay and my grandson Michael. Dave would drive up from Topeka to take me to lunch at the Red Lobster at 95th and Metcalf in Overland Park, KS. He kept me in stitches laughing about his take on events. He was funnier than Jay Leno and David Letterman but their lives were so different.

I once told my daughter Elizabeth that Dave Holloway was just as brilliant as my genius brother Pat, but because of the tragedy of his mental illness, he would never have the achievements of my brother, a much beloved law professor for forty-five years at Creighton University School of Law. "Heaven is Real" says that seven year old author with the experience in heaven. A film has been made of his book. Dave Holloway must have a really high place in heaven.

I still had trouble focusing my eyes when the book Dave sent me came in the mail, but I was able to strain to read portions of this book. It contained a chapter on how lithium causes excessive weight gain. I panicked since I had already gained weight when I was bulimic after the death of my three male friends in 1982 and I stopped the vomiting but not the compulsive eating at the time. I had lost some of that weight, but not all of it.

Sundance and Cherokee Moon

Someone I know had stomach stapling surgery, so I contacted the same doctor and had the surgery. I suffered a lot with the post operative pain for over a month, and I never lost any weight from the surgery as other people had.

After recovery I went to a Marian conference in Wichita, Kansas, with mother, Karen, Rosemary, her mother, and her cousin Dorothy in a van and all the way there we could all see the Miracle of the Sun. Later some of us went to a Marian conference in Des Moines, Iowa. We met Father Halley and Father Bill there as well. They had been in Wichita too. During the afternoon session in Des Moines, someone shouted: "It's the Miracle of the Sun. I can see the Miracle of the Sun!" The room nearly emptied while 300 people saw the Miracle of the Sun. The next morning, the *Des Moines Register* reported this fact and about the Marian conference with Russian mystic Joseph Turelya, a gulag prisoner in Russia for twenty years who stood in for Medjugorje visionary Ivan who was not able to come from Medjugorje. Joseph Turelya warned us about Russia reverting.

Sometime during this period, international healing priest Fr. Peter Mary Rookey, OSM, who held healing services at the Wichita conference, and Fr. Bill celebrated Mass together and held a joint healing service at Immaculate Conception Church in Omaha. This would be the first of a number of Father Rookey's healing services I would attend in four states, Nebraska, Iowa, Illinois and Missouri. I had many people to pray for who needed healing.

Father Rookey sent out a monthly newsletter from his International Compassionate Ministry reporting all the miracle healings people had obtained from the Lord and the Blessed Mother after Father blessed them and prayed for them. In one of the newsletters, Father told of a miracle that was happening in the Servite Church in Chicago. During the consecration of the Communion host and the wine into the body and blood of Jesus, an image of the Blessed Mother holding the baby Jesus in light would appear on the huge portrait of Saint Juliana, a Servite saint, hanging above the altar. As soon as Communion was over, the image disappeared.

Helen, Mary Ann and I traveled to Chicago to attend Father Rookey's Mass and to see the miracle. We were amazed. Just as Father had explained in the newsletter as soon as he blessed the Communion host and the wine, the image of the Blessed Mother with the baby Jesus appeared on the huge portrait of St. Juliana hanging on the wall way up behind the altar.

129

Their images were all made with light. We became witnesses to this miracle. Father Rookey is over 100 years old now and in retirement and unable to travel, but I have no doubt that he will be beatified and canonized a saint in the Catholic Church after his death.

CHAPTER 8: ANOTHER VISION AND INNER SPEAKING

As I told you earlier, in the summer of 1990, Rosemary and I, after lunch together downtown, were driving up Martha Street to Immaculate Conception Church because I had told her that from the back the church looked just like the back of St. James Church in Medjugorje. Every one who has gone to Medjugorje has great affection for St. James Church. For a number of years the apparitions of the Blessed Mother took place there.

I told you that Rosemary and I saw a grey cloud as we were approaching 24th Street, and were alarmed that there was a fire up there and that the Immaculate Conception Church might be involved. When we got up near the top of the hill, we saw that it was a grey cloud just above us not up in the sky and as it started to move south down 24th street past the church, we followed it up toward Vinton and back north toward the church again behind a commercial center. The street we were on stopped so we turned around and went back the way we came. When the Blessed Mother appeared to the visionaries, she appeared with a grey cloud at her feet.

While we were driving I got that inner locution or inner speaking that the Blessed Mother was coming to Omaha with Ivan at Immaculate Conception Church. We remembered that in Medjugorje we were told that the Blessed Mother often appeared to the visionaries with a grey cloud at her feet and we wondered if she was with that cloud and if she was blessing the church and the area around it. Rosemary and I went to the rectory and told Father Bill about the cloud and my inner speaking. He said to be in prayer and we shouldn't tell anyone but let the Blessed Mother arrange the visit.

Well, years later I took Rosemary's deposition in my personal injury case where I was hurt at a Hy-Vee grocery store in Overland Park, Kansas. The store employee left a cart full of ice to melt causing me to hydroplane and fall on my spine. During my deposition, the lawyer on the other side was trying to make me out as crazy because I was bi-polar. So I deposed Rosemary and questioned her about Medjugorje and about the incident with the grey cloud, my inner speaking and the Blessed Mother's visit to Omaha.

Rosemary, like me, is an attorney. Under oath, she confirmed everything we had experienced, the grey cloud, following it, my inner speaking that the Blessed Mother was coming to Omaha with Ivan to Immaculate Conception Church, and the fact that we went to Father Bill and he told us not to tell anyone but to let the Blessed Mother work out the details. I still have that deposition. I lost the slip and fall case against Hy-Vee because no jury in Johnson County, Kansas had ever found for a plaintiff in a slip and fall case, but the deposition of Rosemary was worth the effort. Ed Fogarty came down to Kansas City, Kansas to testify for me as well.

CHAPTER 9: THE BLESSED MOTHER ACCEPTS OUR INVITATION

.

Nearly two years after Rosemary and I saw the grey cloud, I got a phone call from Helen. Father Bill learned that Ivan was coming to Omaha on December 7th, 1991, the feast day observance of the feast of the Immaculate Conception. The feast day is December 8th, but because the 8th was on a Sunday, the feast was observed on the 7th. Ivan and his interpreter were staying with the Intercessors of the Lamb, the same religious group that sponsored our pilgrimages to Medjugorje. If you saw the movie 'The Song of Bernadette,' you would know that the Blessed Mother told Bernadette that she was the Immaculate Conception.

I asked Father Bill if I should tell the Intercessors that Ivan should be at Immaculate Conception Church. Father said "No, let the Blessed Mother guide them." They chose Immaculate Conception for the Mass and Ivan's talk. The 4:30 p.m. apparition of the Blessed Mother to Ivan took place at the Intercessors of the Lamb's facility. Rosemary and her mother Teresa were in a room nearby. Teresa, who speaks many languages, heard the conversation between the Blessed Mother and Ivan, and shared what she heard with us. It was a special gift to Rosemary's mother Teresa.

CHAPTER 10: THE CELEBRATION AT IMMACULATE CONCEPTION CHURCH

Ivan, then about 24 years old, was interviewed by the religion reporter for the *Omaha World Herald* newspaper about his visit and his apparitions from the Blessed Mother. The paper ran the story and a picture of Ivan. That night the Mass was said together by Father Bill and Father Halley and two other priests. After Mass, Father Bill, in his introduction for Ivan, told how "Father Halley and Mary Kay Green and others in 1988 took a key to the City of Omaha to invite the Blessed Mother and the visionaries to come to Omaha and three years later she has come with Ivan."

Ivan through an interpreter told the story of the early apparitions and Our Lady's messages. Afterward, Father Bill, holding a microphone like TV host Phil Donahue, led a question and answer session with members of the congregation and Ivan and his interpreter. I have the video and audio of the Mass, Father's introduction, Ivan's talk and the question and answer period. My mother, my daughter Mary Kay and her two year old son Michael and I were present for this celebration. Over a thousand people crammed into the small church.

After everything was over, I took Michael up to be blessed by Father Bill. Father blessed him and then he bent toward Michael and whispered in his ear. All of a sudden Michael started clapping his hands. I have always wondered what Father said to Michael that made him so happy. He had been crying during the ceremony.

CHAPTER 11: SEEKING A NEW DOCTOR

After my inner speakings were confirmed by the Blessed Mother's apparition in Omaha and our invitation to her confirmed by Father Bill in the audio and video of the Blessed Mother's visit to Omaha with Ivan, I sought a new psychiatrist. Because of the reaction of the two doctors at Cherokee, I did not tell any of my Omaha psychiatrists about my spiritual experiences. But then, I went to Dr. Jack Wisman, M.D. He is the only psychiatrist after the two doctors at Cherokee that I told about my spiritual experiences until I told my current psychiatrist Dr. A.M. Mirza, M.D. Like I did with my other doctors, I have seen Dr. Mirza every three months. I have seen him for ten years for fifteen minutes at a time here in the Kansas City area since 2004. It is amazing what a great doctor/patient and friend relationship you can have with someone for only fifteen minutes at a time every three months. The insurance companies and Medicare mandate the fifteen minutes. I cherish Dr. Mirza. I trust him with my life.

After seeing Dr. Wisman, M.D. for months, and meeting with his social worker, I expressed my curiosity if I was put on lithium and the other psychiatric meds because of my religious experiences or if I was truly bi-polar. I never intentionally went off my medications because Father Bill at all his healing services repeatedly told us if you think you have had a healing never to go off medication unless a doctor tells you. Like I told you, he said that God works through doctors.

I met Dr. Wisman while we were both attending Unity Church in the early 1980's. It was there that I learned to meditate again and met my friend Carole Barnes. Dr. Wisman had his associate psychologist Dr. Joseph Stankus, Ph.D. give me a battery of psychological tests including the MMPI, (Minnesota Multi-phasic Personality Inventory) and I passed them all showing that I was not psychotic because I had these extraordinary spiritual experiences. I was on lithium and other medications since Cherokee, and my spiritual experiences continued on medication. I asked him if I could go off of lithium because of the test results. Dr. Wisman agreed and asked me to come back in a month which I completely forgot.

Way before that Doctor Wisman asked me what I wanted to do with my life. I told him that I always wanted to be a writer. He suggested that I could work with his social worker, a very nice man whose name I cannot remember, and that I could recapture memories for the book I wanted to write, a memoir. After every session with the social worker, I came home and wrote and wrote as the memories flowed. I even gave a title to my book which included my years on the City Council: **Bob Kerrey's Nebraska, Warren Buffett's Omaha and My Home Too** which I based on former Chicago Mayor Jane Byrne's memoir titled **My Chicago**. It was about my life in Omaha and my City Council years. The month after Dr.Wisman let me go off of lithium, I wrote furiously. Using the positive affirmation technique I learned at Unity, I put a sign on the inside of my door with the dollars I would earn from this book, thousands of dollars.

Not realizing I was in a full blown mania, I wanted to go to Iowa again to see Senator Hughes. Without a car, I went to a free clinic to find a person to drive me to Des Moines. I had money to pay for the trip. Eventually I thumbed a ride with a union leader I knew who took me to Steven's Center a center that provides food, meals and shelter to people in need. I was looking for a driver there to take me to Des Moines (A few years later I ran into that union man again, and he told me he had contacted my brother because of the way I was talking. He told me his ex-wife was bi-polar and he recognized the rapid speech symptom).

When I got to Steven's Center, I recognized the director from my old neighborhood and told her what I needed. She said she would find someone to take me to Iowa. She had me wait there for the longest time. It seemed like forever, when my two brothers showed up with a woman police officer to have me go to the hospital. I asked them to let me call Dr. Wisman because he had taken me off lithium and I wanted to see him. They agreed to let me call him. I called Dr. Wisman and he refused to see me. He just refused flat out. He didn't say: "Go with them and I will meet you at the hospital." He just refused to see me. I felt betrayed by him.

The woman officer approached me to pat me down, something the sheriff's deputies in Akron, Iowa, never did. I had never been patted down in my life, and to prevent it, I pulled down my slacks and was half naked much to the shock of my brothers who shielded their faces with their hands. Needless to say, the police officer did not pat me down. I had nothing in my slacks or elsewhere.

I was taken to the St. Joseph Mental Hospital locked ward. The hospital was a multi-storied modern building. Late that night I couldn't sleep and went into the little dining area in the ward and another patient was there.

Sundance and Cherokee Moon

He told me he had a radio in his head and that he was told to give me this piece of paper. It was a crumpled pamphlet. It was a copy of the statement of patient's rights: the right to have a hearing within seven days, and the right to have a lawyer from the Public Defender's office represent me if I couldn't afford a lawyer. It also mentioned that you could stay voluntarily for two weeks if you waived a hearing. I had not been given one of these pamphlets. This man may be mentally ill, I thought, but his radio communication is real.

The next day Rosemary came to see me after I called her. By this time I was angry and highly irritable and there was extreme tension in my voice. Rosemary said I was rational but she noted how my voice sounded and she cautioned me to accept the two weeks. I agreed to stay voluntarily and the hearing was cancelled. I sent with her a letter to all my family that I was going to sue them for trying to commit me. Needless to say, none of them came to visit me, except my brother Pat and his wife Barbara. He claims to this day that I said they were robots. I don't remember this and can't imagine why I called them robots.

As an aside, Nebraska's Mental Health Commitment Law provides for an administrative hearing at the place where you are being held. This was the same in Iowa. Many states require a hearing in a court room before a judge for commitment; this is called a judicial hearing.

In 1980, I had developed a medical condition which at that time had no name. Pain anywhere in my body, including psychic pain causing physical symptoms, caused my body to go into paralysis starting with my feet and causing unconsciousness as the paralysis came all the way up to my head. Many years later, I went back to my heart specialist Dr. James Morgan, M.D. in the 1990's and I learned that the condition now had a name, Vaso-Vagal Syncope, and that they even had a test to confirm it, a table top test after an injection of a stimulant, and they even had a medicine to treat it, Atenolol.

But at St. Joseph's hospital, I was dehydrated and severely constipated (a common side effect from psychiatric medications) and in straining, I suffered on a scale of ten, number 10 pain and the paralysis started. I slid to the floor. I thought I was going to die. Years later, after several more years of these "attacks" I realized that if I died, it would be from hitting my head while I fell down in pain. (On one occasion the pain was so great and I suffered so much pain from turning my ankle that I fell face first on a brick sidewalk near the law school and my face looked like a truck ran over it for weeks.)

So at St. Joe's, I reached for my rectum and with a finger put some stool on the bathroom wall to let people know what had caused my death. I don't know how long I was unconscious (on one occasion I was able to time the unconsciousness at thirty minutes by looking at my watch as the pain hit and looking at it again when I became conscious) but eventually someone on staff came to get me and put me to bed. No one asked me what had happened. I was treated like a child, not a child, but a mental patient. My blood pressure was not taken, my pulse was not taken, and no flash light was shined into my eyes. I was given no medical treatment. It was assumed that I was acting out. (In 1980, during a canoe trip to the Niobrara River, I had a similar bout of unconsciousness while straining and ended up in the hospital there.)

The next day Dr. Wisman came and he proceeded to scold me about the stool on the wall incident. He didn't ask me what happened. You have to know that there were monitors in our rooms and staff looked at us from a desk somewhere in the unit. Apparently they couldn't see in the bathroom, or, could they? At any rate, someone hadn't been very attentive and when they found me they just assumed that I was acting out. As I told you before, at Cherokee, the doctors treated the physical and the mental.

This was the second time Dr.Wisman had failed me. When I got out of the hospital, I went to another psychiatrist. My life would have taken another course if I had stayed with Dr. Wisman and expressed my anger. It doesn't really matter which choice I made because either way for an author good things and bad things are all good material, drama is drama. Both paths would have given me material for this book. I am happy with the choice I made. By the way, I had filled eighteen legal pads in writing my book <u>Bob Kerrey's Nebraska, Warren Buffet's Omaha and My Home Too</u>. I figure that would be about 300 pages typed at two handwritten pages for one typed page, a completed book.

Years later, as I previously noted, when I got all my hospital records, I learned that the doctors at Cherokee had originally given me a dual diagnosis: Bi-Polar and Schizo-Affective. The definition of Schizo-Affective disorder is seeing things that are not there. They had taken my vision of Jesus on the Cross, the Blessed Mother and St. Therese as a symptom of Schizo-Affective disorder. At the same time I got my records from St. Joseph, and learned that Dr.Wisman had only diagnosed me Bi-Polar. He had accepted my spiritual experiences as real. After being at St. Joe's under Dr. Wisman's care, I learned that you could be mentally ill and at the same time have extraordinary spiritual experiences. They were not mutually exclusive. After St. Joseph Mental Hospital, I could no longer question my bi-polar diagnosis.

For a couple of years, I was afraid to read any of my words on those eighteen yellow legal pads for fear that they would be irrational because of my hospitalization. One day I started writing the book over and I randomly grabbed one of the legal pads from the box of eighteen. The two legal pads were identical word for word except one was in the third person and one was in the first person. I started pulling out other pads. I realized that I had not numbered the pads. I was frustrated about the amount of work it would take to put them in order. I saved them, but started to work on another book called *Two Lawyers in Love*
.

I sent a query letter to Jay Garon, John Grisham's agent. He wrote me back and said he wasn't interested in *Two Lawyers in Love*, but I should send him anything else I wrote. Before I could write him again, he died. The story of *The Story of Bob Kerrey's Nebraska, Warren Buffett's Omaha and My Home Too* was sad too, because when my daughters were moving me to Kansas City years later in 2003, I let them throw away my box containing my book. I sorely regret that decision, but I was convinced I would never have an opportunity to publish it. Oh, well, maybe someday I could write it again.

And I am thinking of changing the name of my novel *Two Lawyers in Love* to *Lunch*. It is a fictional novel based upon my eight years of friendship with my beloved mentor Arthur O'Leary conducted at lunch once a week for eight years until his death in 1982.

Or I might expand the number of lawyers who befriended me and served as mentors and friends to include my former bosses Ben Wall and Ernest Wintroub, my former boss Judge Joseph Moylan, my friend former Judge Bill Staley with whom I worked for Judge Moylan and Judge Colleen Buckley and my friends attorney Tom Walsh and his wife Virginia and my friend attorney Sally Rau. I would call this book *The Cheerleaders*.

I could write a book about my two years as a law clerk. That could be three different fiction books or non-fiction books, but preferably three books of fiction covering my first ten years of practicing law. I already wrote the fictionalized screenplay about my three years of law school at Creighton University Law School in Omaha in the first large class of women, thirty of one hundred and eighty freshmen, and the first class with mothers called: *They Let Mothers in Law School?* Then I would have four legal fiction books. I wrote the screenplay in the 1990's and I will publish it after publishing this book. It is being typed on the computer. I didn't have a computer when I first wrote it.

The study group we formed the first week of law school was comprised of Jeanie Daly, Annette Mason and me. We were all mothers. Jeanie was a divorced mother of two girls, Annette was married with a new baby girl and I was a single mother of my twin girls Elizabeth and Mary Kay. Later in the year, we mothers extended our group to include my friend Mike Boyle, married to Anne and the father of five kids, and another classmate Phil Brooks.

Years later Mike would become Mayor of Omaha and my classmates Walt Calinger, Brenda Council and Fred Conley would follow me and become elected to the Omaha City Council. The five of us from our law school class would be elected to the city government, and Walt Calinger would be both a City Council Member and Mayor. We all took Municipal Law together from our friend Professor Richard Shugrue.

CHAPTER 12: THE KANSAS YEARS

The new psychiatrist I chose was named William Egan, M.D. I had become familiar with him years before when I represented a very nice woman who wanted to fire her psychiatrist. She was in St. Joseph's Mental Hospital. She called me. She wanted to go to William Egan. Her psychiatrist became so irrational that he told me: "She has no rights, mental patients have no rights." He ordered her file locked up with an order that I was not to have access to it. I had to go to the head legal counsel for the hospital to get that doctor off her case and let Dr. Egan treat her.

At that first meeting with Dr. Egan, I told him why I chose him—because my client had so much respect for him. He told me that he and the other doctor had been in practice together and were terminating that relationship at the time of my client's hospitalization.

I shared my concern that my family members who had no regular contact with me kept hospitalizing me, and my feelings about Dr. Wisman's role. The Mental Health Commitment Law required the person who filed the complaint to have seen the alleged mentally ill person near that time. No one in my family had seen me on a regular basis except my mother and she did not file the commitment papers, my sister a deputy county attorney filed the complaint and she had not seen me in months. The second session I had with Dr. Egan, he said to me: "Miss Green, I have been thinking about your situation, and I highly recommend that you move away from your family."

A week or so later my daughter Mary Kay was being transferred to Lenexa, KS. with Coca Cola, and she asked me to move with her and my grandson Michael. She respected my desire to write and arranged to have Michael in day care half a day while I watched him at night until she got off. It was in Lenexa that I tried to write again *Bob Kerrey's Nebraska, Warren Buffetts' Omaha and My Home Too and Two Lawyers in Love.*

One evening, I took Michael with me to pick Mary Kay up from work. This time we went into the plant. I got to see the offices and the plant and the night workers. Upon questioning Mary Kay, it was clear to me that the jobs in that Coca Cola distribution center were race and sex segregated. I told her that this violated the law. The drivers were all white males, the truck loaders, a lower paying job, were all black males, and women were segregated into lower paying clerical positions. I encouraged her to file a charge with the EEOC.

About this time, I had not been able to get a hold of my friend Bertha Griggs. I called my mother after an unusual week of not talking to her, she told me that Bertha had been trying to get a hold of me because her mother had a stroke and had been in a coma, and when she came out of the coma, the only person she was asking for was me. Mother gave me Bertha's number and apologized because she hadn't called me but explained that she could not remember my phone number.

I got a hold of Bertha in Kansas City, Missouri, and she asked me to come up to Omaha with her to see her mother in the hospital. I went in first and went up to her: "Carrie, Carrie, what's the matter? The nurses are worried about you because you have been asking for me every day all day long?"

"I met your father," she said very seriously. I looked at her stunned: "But my father has been dead for thirty-six years." "Not here," she said pointing down. "Up there," she pointed up. She then told me that she had died and all her relatives were there and so was my father. Then she started to sob. I asked her why she was crying. She said he had a message for me and she couldn't remember it. "Carrie, this is something happy. My father's in heaven and he's asking about me." Actually, the message had to be for all of us, but my first reaction was that it was for me.

Now there were two things I didn't tell you about this event. First of all, my friend Bertha, her ex-husband, her children and her mother are all African Americans. At the time Bertha and her mother had over two hundred living black relatives. My father and mother are white as are all my siblings. My girls are white. I have bi-racial nieces and my grandchildren are bi-racial. But my father would have stuck out in that crowd of Bertha's black relatives up in heaven.

Second, I never spoke of my father to Carrie. I don't even know if she knew he was alive or dead. The third thing about this story is that my friend Bertha Griggs died around 2000 from a massive stroke. Her mother just died recently in 2014, and I taped her last year where she affirmed that incident when she died and went to heaven and met my father.

I worked on another book while I lived in Kansas in the mid 1990's. By this time Mary Kay, Michael and I were living in a duplex in Overland

Sundance and Cherokee Moon

Park, Kansas. My friend Bertha Griggs (an R.N. nurse with master degrees in counseling and gerontology and a divorce), had moved to Kansas City, Missouri, a few years earlier with her twin children, a son Shaumma and a daughter Bena. Bena and Shaumma were twins a year younger than my twins. We had been neighbors and friends in Omaha for fifteen years.

Bertha had been hired in Kansas City, Missouri, by Swope Ridge Nursing Home and was in charge of developing an Alzheimer's unit for the home. She showed me all around the facility. Bertha had a theory that exercise would improve cognition in Alzheimer's patients just like it does for non-affected persons. The key stone of her unit was an indoor walking track about the size of five or six rooms. We walked the tract.

In moving the patients into their new rooms in the unit, Bertha and her son took photographs of everything in each patient's room, and perfectly duplicated those rooms in the new unit so that the patients would not become disoriented and disturbed. She also established guidelines for staff— compassionate, but no finger nail polish and no jewelry to distract the patients.

I told her we should write a book about developing her unit and the staff for it. I told her that I would ask her a series of questions from what she had just told me and that I would ask her those questions and receive her answers just like a legal deposition or sworn statement under oath to tell the truth. I prepared the questions and tape recorded the session with her and blended the questions into her answers so that the written book would all be her speaking. We called it *The Alzheimer's Project.*

Bertha even drew up the plans for a nursing home that she wanted to start. The home was a circular building with patients' rooms around the exterior walls. Inside were glass windows in a circle and on the inside of those windows in the center of the circle was a day care center. Patients who were able could "grandparent" the children. Other patients could delight in watching the children play and learn. She copyrighted the plan.

As I told you, Bertha died around 2000. She died weeks after that massive stroke. I was too ill to leave Omaha to come to see her before she died or to come to her funeral. My daughters went to see her in the hospital and sent my love and talked to her believing she could hear. She was in a coma. They went to her funeral too.

143

Sundance and Cherokee Moon

The actress Debra Winger had written an article for one of the women's magazines about the time she was in a coma. She said that she heard everything that people said to her. Reading that article and telling my girls about it was the reason they talked to Bertha while she was in a coma.

Years later, after I had lived again in Omaha for a few years and had returned down south again living this time in Kansas City, Missouri, with my daughter Elizabeth, I contacted the nursing home for permission to come there and take pictures of the walking track. The new director knew nothing about it. Apparently they had turned the track into patient rooms. This was tragic economics because a number of years after she died, research was published showing that exercise improved the brain functioning of Alzheimer's patients. Bertha Griggs was a pioneer. Bertha was more than a pioneer. She was one of my friends to whom God talked. She called her inner voice "The Spirit," and she was totally obedient to "The Spirit." When she died she had been a divinity student at the St. Paul Seminary in Kansas City, Missouri.

Bertha felt her new vocation was to minister to gay, lesbian, bi-sexual and transgender people. She herself entered into a commitment ceremony with a younger woman named Dorothy. When she called me to tell me she was getting married and asked me to be her bridesmaid, I said I would but I asked her why she was getting married. She told me: "Dorothy is younger than me and she has promised to take care of me if I become ill and die."

A few years earlier, a doctor at the University of Nebraska Medical Center had caused Bertha to suffer heart damage when he gave her medication listed on her medical chart as prohibited. She never sued because she was a nurse, but her heart medications alone cost over $800.00/month out of pocket and until she worked at Swope Ridge, she had to come up with the money every month.

BOOK IV: THE SCENT OF ROSES AND ANGELS

CHAPTER 13: SHARED SPIRITUAL EXPERIENCES

One of my sister's mother-in-law, and also my friend, lives in Kansas City, Missouri. Her name is Edith West, and she is called "Lassie," or "Grandma Lassie." She is a delightful curmudgeon of a woman. My sister's late husband had grown up in Kansas City and had moved to Omaha to go to school. Lassie told me that she had been told she had cancer. She refused to go back to the doctor. I told her about Father Rookey, the healing priest from Chicago, and that I had attended his healing services in Wichita and Omaha. He was scheduled to go to Sioux City, Iowa, for a Healing Mass. I invited her to go with me. She agreed.

Now Lassie is African American and raised in the AME Methodist Church. But for years she took care of the elderly mother of a large Catholic family. A couple of the daughters went to Medjugorje and brought Lassie a rosary from Medjugorje blessed by the Blessed Mother, so she was familiar with Catholicism and Medjugorje. I told her that Father Peter Mary Rookey, this Chicago healing priest, goes to Medjugorje every year. She knew that I had taken my mother to Medjugorje.

We drove up to Omaha in my little white truck. (The truck is a story in itself. A woman I knew from St. Margaret Mary's told me she had been told by the Lord to sell me her truck. All she asked for it was $200.00. She insisted that I buy it. It was an older truck but it was really a gift not a sale at that price.) We picked up my friend Karen in Omaha and drove up to Sioux City. I brought with me a medium sized bottle of water and a medium sized bottle with virgin olive oil in it to have Father Rookey bless them during the Mass. But miracle of miracles we ran into Father in the parking lot and he not only blessed the water and the oil, he blessed all of us, and he let someone take a picture of us with him.

After Mass, Father asked everyone who wanted a healing to come up onto the altar and form two lines on either side of the alter. Lassie didn't want to go up although she came for a healing. "I'll stand in for you," I told her. When Father came to me and laid his hand on my head, I immediately fell backward caught by a catcher, a man who caught me and laid me on the marble floor. I had this tremendous feeling of peace and all I saw with my eyes closed was pure white. This phenomenon is called being slain in the spirit. Father Rookey is a Charismatic priest like Father Whelan and Father Halley.

That night we drove back to Omaha and all three of us stayed with my long time Lutheran and Unity friend Carole Barnes in Council Bluffs, Iowa, a city just directly across the Missouri river from Omaha. In the morning, I told Carole about meeting Father Rookey and of him blessing my bottle of water and bottle of virgin olive oil. She asked to see them. "Let's bless each other with them," she said. I picked up the bottle with the oil in it and opened the cap. Immediately the whole five room apartment filled with the scent of fresh cut roses. Right away I put in a call to Father Rookey in Chicago hoping he would be back. He answered. (You could call his International Healing Ministry and get volunteers to answer the phone and take your prayer petitions for Father Rookey or you can email them to him, but to get him answering your call is a minor miracle because so many people try to call him.) (He is retired now due to his age and health.)

I reminded Father that we had met him in the parking lot of the church in Sioux City and that he had blessed the bottles of water and virgin olive oil I brought with me. "Father, I am in Council Bluffs, Iowa, now staying with a friend and I just opened the bottle of blessed oil and the entire five room apartment immediately filled with the scent of roses. What does that mean?"

Father replied: "That's a sign that the Blessed Mother is present with you." He asked how many of us were there. I said four of us. He told me: "Go out and buy five small bottles of virgin olive oil, pour out one forth of the oil from the five bottles into a container, then pour into the four bottles enough of the original oil to fill to the top, and finally pour the rest of the oil into the original bottle still with oil in it. All the oil will be blessed that way." We were all amazed and felt very blessed.
Lassie and I said goodbye to Carole and took Karen home in Omaha and headed back to Kansas City. Lassie announced that she had been cured. She is still alive today in 2015 and just had her 83th birthday this past year.

A month or so later, Carole called me and begged me to represent her daughter in a custody suit filed by her ex-husband. Apparently this was the second or third custody suit he had filed against her since the divorce. He

Sundance and Cherokee Moon

forced her into bankruptcy and didn't win one of the cases but she couldn't afford to hire a lawyer now.

I told Carole that I didn't think I could ever go back into a court room again because the stress would be too great with my bi-polar illness. She begged me and begged me. The trial was set for Monday July 5th that year. I came up to stay with Carole for the hearing. On Saturday the 3rd we drove to Schuyler, Nebraska, where Father Bill Whelan had been transferred to St. Augustine Parish. We were going to visit with him and have him pray for Carole's daughter and her children. Father said he would. He also blessed three black rosaries I had bought, one for Carole, one for her daughter, also Lutheran like her mother, and one for me.

While we were there Father pointed out an article in the **Omaha World Herald** about the miracle two law partners had. Larry Corrigan went to the hospital to visit his friend and partner Tom Dowd who was in there for cancer treatment. He told Tom he was going to go out and put a bet on a horse race. Tom gave him some money and told him to bet for him too. When Larry came back to the hospital to give Tom his winnings, Larry had a heart attack in Tom's room. Tom's wife Sally grabbed a wheel chair and pushed Larry across the hospital to the emergency room and saved his life. If Larry had gone home he would have died because his wife Sancha was out of town. Next, Tom was cured of the cancer. I told Father that Tom and Larry and their wives were friends of mine and they were on the list of 500 people I took to Medjugorje to pray for.

When we got back to Omaha from Schuyler, it was time for Father Halley's Saturday night prayer group at St. Margaret Mary's. I wanted to introduce Carole to him, have him pray for her daughter and the children, and also bless the three black rosaries. Father did and he blessed us too. This was Saturday, July 3rd 1993 or 1994.

That night I became so tired that I went to bed early. I must have been comatose because Carole told me the next morning that she had to call the police three times on her neighbors because of all the fireworks they set off. I hadn't heard a thing. Then she told me that she had this spiritual experience. She saw angels all around her house.

Monday July 5th, Carole stayed outside the court room while I represented her daughter inside. This was only one of three court rooms at the time that had clear glass doors. I was able to negotiate a settlement with the ex-

147

husband's lawyer for custody and increased child support. When we left the court room, Carole told us that while she was watching everything through the glass door, the area filled with the scent of roses. The Blessed Mother was present again.

When I went back to Kansas, I took my grandson Michael to see the movie *Angels in the Outfield* with Danny Glover. The angels in the movie were made of light in the form of beings with wings and flowing robes. I called Carole in Council Bluffs that night and told her about the movie. "Go see the movie and tell me if the angels in the movie resemble the angels you saw."

Carole had described her angels as beings of light with wings. She took her grandson Aaron to the movie, and called me that night. "They are the same as my angels" she reported, "only my angels were as tall as my building." We were amazed. Carole lived in a two story building.

While I was in Omaha again later, our other friend named Carol, Carol Kangior who had gone to see Wayne Dyer with me in 1980, called to talk to me. She had heard from Carole about the blessed oil and the Blessed Mother being in Carole's apartment. She told me: "My son Matthew is in a coma. Will you bring the oil and go with us to pray with him." I met Carol and her daughters in Matthew's room at the hospital. I took some of the oil from the bottle and made little crosses on his forehead, on both hands, on his side and on his feet, all the places where Jesus was wounded on the cross. Then we all prayed out loud for Matthew saying the Our Father and other prayers. Carol and her family are Protestant.

Two days later Carol called me. "Matthew came out of the coma this morning, Mary Kay. It's a miracle." It was truly amazing. I do not have the gift of healing. God healed Matthew. The anointing with the blessed oil and the prayers must have helped. A few years later I visited with Matthew on the phone. He shared with me that he had a mystical experience a few years after he came out of the coma. It was beautiful he told me.

While I was living in Overland Park, Kansas, I joined Holy Spirit Catholic parish run by the Benedictine priests. Our assistant pastor was very popular with the parishioners. He used to visit with a group of us before daily Mass. On the feast of the Pentecost or Holy Spirit, I was with a few other people with him before the Sunday Mass, and when I went into the church and knelt down for Mass, I got the inner speaking: "He is being called for greater things." Two days later Father Barnabas Senecal was elected Abbott of the province.

One time when I was on my way to Topeka to visit my friend Dave Holloway in the Veterans Hospital there, I made a wrong turn and ended up in Atchison, KS so I stopped at the Abby. Abbott Barnabas was there. He invited me to pray with the monks and to have lunch with them. During lunch, he pointed out one of the monks as being a regular on Mother Angelica's Eternal Word Television Network (EWTN). I admired Mother Angelica for bringing the Mass and the rosary world wide to people including people without priests and people shut in, but she is more conservative than I am. I said: "Let me go talk to him." I don't know what I would have said to him, but the Abbott replied: "You stay here; you are far too liberal for him." I just learned this year that the Abbott retired. He was well revered.

Our duplex in Overland Park was within walking distance to the library and to a multi-plex movie theater in a major shopping center. I used the library frequently researching all the movies, books and current events during 1974 through 1982, the years I had lunch once a week with my beloved friend and mentor Arthur O'Leary. We always discussed these things at lunch along with some of the cases we were working on. This friendship was the actual source of the fictional book I was writing titled *Two Lawyers in Love*. I fictionalized our friendship. It wasn't a romance, but we truly cared for each other. I did all my research at that library. The so called experts are wrong. You can have close personal relationships between men and women that are not affairs. I had many male lawyer friends and some of whom were married. I liked all of their wives. And I had men and women mentors.

Helen was one of my women mentors. She was responsible for my being chosen as one of the summer White House interns where I was stationed at the Treasury Department and participating in the weekly sessions at Constitution Hall with all the other summer interns and hearing President Kennedy, Attorney General Robert F. Kennedy and the other cabinet members talk to us each week about considering careers in the federal government.

And it was Helen while working in the Attorney General's office who introduced me to John Doar who hired me to work in the Civil Rights

Division. It was Helen who told me I must keep my girls because I had a right to and it was she and her husband George who gave me the money to keep my girls. It was Helen who invited my mother and me to attend Father Whelan's healing Masses. It was Helen who encouraged my mother and me to start attending the Medjugorje Masses at St. Margaret Mary's. It was Helen following the statements from the Lord to her who lent my mother and me the money to go to Medjugorje. Helen has been my friend since I was eighteen years old and working on John F. Kennedy's Presidential campaign with her as executive secretary of the campaign the summer before I went into the convent. She was close to my late father and my late mother and my family.

Back in Overland Park, to get a seat in the multi-plex theater, you had to arrive at least thirty minutes ahead of time. Since I was going to the movies by myself, I used that time to pray for all my favorite actors and actresses and people in the entertainment business. I was grateful for their shared talent but understood from all I read about them and about the pressures and temptations they were subjected to, such as drug and alcohol addictions, that they needed prayers. And of course I always started my prayers for Elizabeth Taylor and Robert Redford, my favorite modern movie stars.

The Nebraska Mental Health Law only listed two specific mental illnesses, namely, drug addiction and alcoholism. The law did not name any other specific illness such as bi-polar illness, schizophrenia, depression, anxiety disorder or any other mental illness. I was impressed that the Nebraska Unicameral was enlightened enough to recognize that alcoholism and drug addiction are mental illnesses and as we now know all mental illnesses are really brain chemistry illnesses whatever their genetic or emotional triggers.

Before I moved to Kansas with my daughter Mary Kay, I reconnected with one of my dear friends from law school, a brilliant younger woman who at the top of her career was appointed to a panel of lawyers to oversee federal multi-district airplane disaster lawsuits. After that she had succumbed to raging alcoholism and was potentially suicidal. She used to call me every day in Kansas from Omaha, and weekly sent me bouquets of roses. I thanked her for the roses but insisted she didn't need to send them to me. I treasured the phone calls because they were proof she was still alive. A year or so later, she was arrested on her fourth DUI and her lawyer worked it out with the court to let her serve her one year sentence in a mental hospital.

I came back to Omaha the year she was hospitalized, and I visited her frequently. She immediately returned to drinking after she was released. Red wine was her downfall. During the time after her release, she wrote a book, a civil rights murder mystery book. It was brilliant. She let me read it. But after this she called me one night and announced she was going to kill herself. I lived more than thirty minutes away. I always take such threats as real. I called the police to go help her. They found her in a very bad state and took her with them to hospitalize her. They called and let me know she was in pretty bad shape. She told me later that the police drove her around all night trying to find a mental hospital with a vacant bed. The county hospital finally took her in. At her hearing, the board of mental health committed her. She went to a state hospital rather than a private one on her trust fund. Her father had been a wealthy attorney.

She was pretty good for awhile and eventually moved out of state, dying at a young age of pulmonary edema and she left a number of young children who were living with her ex-husband. Her last years were so tragic. I mourned her. Alcoholism and drug addiction are such insidious illnesses and so is mental illness.

Not too long ago, drug companies had to suspend their trials on medications that hopefully controlled the diseases of drug addiction and alcoholism by impacting the pleasure centers of the brain. They had to suspend the trials because the drugs eliminated all feelings of pleasure and joy and as a result too many people were committing suicide.

I had additional spiritual experiences in Overland Park that I remember in addition to the one about the Abbott. At three o'clock one morning, I was awakened and I knew instinctively that I was to go turn on the television. I put my finger on the remote control and let it scroll until I saw the Reverend Jessie Jackson giving a speech and in the front row was Mrs. Anwar Sadat. Remember, I had seen her speak in Sioux City, Iowa, right after I returned from Medjugorje and Chicago and her name was one of the names I was given to start an international women's prayer group. I realized that she was interested in civil rights as well as international peace. I had also heard Jesse Jackson speak at the Hill Top Projects in Omaha during a Presidential campaign where on top of a dumpster he spoke and raised the aspirations of the women and children in that project. Hill Top Projects were where I had taken the rosaries to the residents and children.

Another time, I woke up at three O'clock a.m. and got out of bed and went into the living room. I put my finger on the remote and I scrolled down and all of a sudden I saw this musical group and the lead singer had a large wooden cross on his back. The screen lit up with the name of the group as Nirvana. I had never heard of them. But I said a rosary for that singer.

A month later on April 5, 1994, I learned that that lead singer was named Kurt Cobain and he died of a heroin overdose. It was also reported that he suffered from severe depression as well as heroin addiction. What a tragedy. What a loss. This year 2015, Nirvana was inducted into the Rock and Roll Hall of Fame. I watched the films of their performances and saw that young, brilliant musician Kurt Cobain.

At the end of 1994, my daughter Mary Kay asked me to go back to Omaha. She was in a relationship. I packed up all my belongings including the box with the eighteen legal pads and my word processor and went to stay with Carole Barnes. I didn't know what I was going to do. Carole found me an apartment and she and her sister and daughter furnished it with some of their own furniture.

Word got out that I was back home, and old clients called me to represent them. I convinced Mary Kay earlier to file a charge of sex discrimination and race discrimination against Coca Cola. When she got her 90 day Right to Sue Letter, a document required by the 1964 Civil Rights Act to allow you to go into federal court before the 90 days is up, the lawyers from Coke down South came to see her. I had not made an appearance in the case. I wasn't practicing law again then. The lawyers told her that if she didn't sue, they guaranteed that things would be better. I told her not to believe them.

On the basis of their promise, she let the 90 Day Right to Sue Letter expire. Then the retaliation started. She called me in Omaha one morning and told me that they had called her into a meeting after lunch, and she was sure that they were going to fire her. "Leave now for lunch and go out and buy a small tape recorder." I urged her. Just as she suspected, they fired her shortly after the 90 days was up. But we had the whole illegal meeting on tape. I had her file a sex, race and retaliation charge with the EEOC and I made my appearance with the agency as her attorney.

I timely filed the case in federal court in Kansas, where she lived, as a class action case, but later I never had the class certified because Ed Fogarty and I decided that just the two of us alone could not handle such a big case against Coca Cola the parent company. It would take a little over a year to get to trial. I handled all the motions and briefs and paper discovery.

When it came time to take the in person depositions or testimony under oath, I asked Ed Fogarty, my lifelong friend and co-counsel on Crystal Chamber's lawsuit, to take the depositions with me and to try the case with me. To shorten the story, after a meeting with the lawyers, we filed a joint Motion for Dismissal. My law student daughter Elizabeth participated in the meeting along with Ed and Mary Kay. I was kept in the car with Elizabeth coming out to me for advice. The Coke lawyers were so mad that I had bested them that it was recommended by the mediator that I not participate.

On a joint Motion to Dismiss by Mary Kay and the representative for Coca Cola, the judge signed an order we prepared dismissing the case with prejudice. Such an order tells the world that both parties were agreeable. Mary Kay next enrolled at Kansas University in Lawrence and graduated with a business degree in accounting. A few years after Mary Kay's case ended, a major law firm in Atlanta filed a class action race and sex discrimination case against Coke and there was a very big settlement.

I was handling a second big case at that time against Mutual of Omaha for three young black women working in the department that processed Medicaid insurance claims. They had protested the brochures showing all black women on the cover and Mutual of Omaha's targeting of only black women to get them to give Mutual rights to handle all their Medicaid claims. Mutual was one of the insurance companies allowed by the federal government to handle Medicaid health claims but they had to enroll the Medicaid recipients. The three women protested and were retaliated against.

Two of the women eventually were successfully represented by an NAACP attorney. And for my remaining client, I did the entire discovery and when it came time for trial I entered into an agreement with Lincoln attorney Thom Cope to be co-counsel with me. Again the lawyers drafted a Motion to Dismiss with Prejudice and an Order for the Judge to sign.

Sundance and Cherokee Moon

When I filed the Mutual case in federal court in Omaha, the newspaper picked up and reported on the case—thus more clients came.

But while I was handling these two cases for clients who could not even afford the court and discovery costs let alone attorneys fees, I took a job from 1:00 p.m. until 9:00 p.m. Monday through Friday to support myself and to pay for the court and discovery costs. I went to work for Warren Buffett at CSI (Central States Indemnity) one of his Berkshire Hathaway insurance companies. At CSI I was licensed to sell credit card and utility payment protection plans. The average length of employment for employees with this company was fifteen days. I lasted for close to a year and only had to quit when it came time to prepare for trial for Mary Kay against Coca Cola.

In addition to pay, CSI provided me group health insurance. This was significant because individual life and health insurance companies routinely denied coverage to people with mental illness. Being barred from health insurance was one of the principle reasons I couldn't go back to work. I couldn't give up my government health insurance. The Affordable Health Care Act or Obama Care, as they call it, now prohibits denial of insurance for pre-existing conditions including mental illness. I have always supported a single payer government sponsored health care system or Medicare for all. When that didn't pass, I supported Obama's Affordable Health Care Act but I still pray for a single payer system in the future.

When I turned sixty-five and received Medicare, I could work again. Before that I tried to get work with the federal government in Kansas City. Kansas City is the city with second largest number of federal employees after Washington, D.C. I even applied for a job with the City of Olathe, Kansas as director of Human Relations, their civil rights office. When I was even denied an interview, I filed a federal discrimination charge with the EEOC. I lost there, and filed pro se or for myself in U.S. District Court for Kansas at Kansas City, Kansas.

After discovery and later mediation with the lawyer for the city and Ed Fogarty (who came down to mediate with me) and me, the attorney for the city and I filed a joint motion to Dismiss with Prejudice. Since Olathe is a government, the settlement is a public record so I can tell you that the case settled. My allegation was that I was denied the job because of my extensive civil rights work as a member of the Omaha City Council and as

154

a civil rights plaintiffs' attorney. I obtained a record in discovery where these facts were mentioned, yet I was denied an interview. My expert witness was the former director of Human Relations for the City of Olathe. He had been the director of the Kansas City Human Relations Department for over twenty years.

Back in Omaha living on 13th Street, I had three additional visions or visual experiences. One morning I woke up and I could see in front of me two rows of floppy disks, three disks in each row. I knew intuitively that I was to go to the word processor. I started typing: 'Why I Am A Civil Rights Lawyer.' The words just flowed out of me. It was automatic writing. By the end of the day, I had written a twenty-five page piece that took me from grade school experiences, to my days at Creighton with Father John Marcoe,
S. J., a faculty member at Creighton University who organized two civil rights groups. The adult group was called the De Porres Club after black saint Martin De Porres. The De Porres Club consisting of black and white members of the community integrated buses, restaurants and places of employment.

The student group, the Society for Social Justice, of which I was a member as was my friend Ed Fogarty, took on the project of documenting racial discrimination in Creighton University approved private student housing. Father Marcoe supervised this project. He had us go out in teams of black and white students. The black students would ask for housing and were told there were no vacancies, and then the white students went to the same houses and were told there was room. We presented our findings to the President of the University, a Jesuit priest, and he threatened to expel us for doing the study. Father Marcoe intervened for us. We were not expelled. The result of the study was that Creighton built two more student dormitories.

The piece covered my time as a clerk in the Civil Rights Division of the United States Department of Justice in Washington, D.C. under Deputy Attorney General John Doar (later chief counsel for the House of Representatives Judiciary Committee in the impeachment proceedings against President Richard Nixon. Hillary Rodman, later Hillary Rodman Clinton, was one of the young lawyers working with him).

The piece covered my days as a government social worker advocating for the rights of my clients, and covered my clerking days with Ben Wall and

155

Sundance and Cherokee Moon

Ernie Wintroub at Wall & Wintroub. There as a senior in law school, I second chaired for Ernie Wintroub a successful major civil rights lawsuit against the City of Omaha Fire Division. The piece covered my civil rights work on the City Council and my civil rights law practice. In all my book writings, I never wrote twenty-five pages in one day. The words just flowed out of me.

It was on 13th Street, that my law student daughter Elizabeth living with me was to be an intern in Washington, D.C. for Nebraska U.S. Senator James Exon. My friend Mary Cornett, who was psychic too, like I was from childhood, had a premonition that Elizabeth should not drive to D.C. It was so strong that she begged her to fly. Elizabeth ignored Mary's entreaties and took off for D.C. in her car. I was in court that day after she left, and when I came home, she had left the following message on my answering machine: "I'm all right now, and I will call you at the next stop."

I called Mary, and we were beside ourselves wondering what "now" meant. At the next stop Elizabeth reported that the string of her tennis shoe got caught in the accelerator pedal, and the car spun around blocking the lane coming toward her. She said she saw a huge truck coming right at her, and closed her eyes knowing she was going to die. When she looked up, the truck was down the highway, and she couldn't understand how it got passed her because she was blocking that entire side of the highway. I was so grateful that she survived this incident.

It was on 13th Street when I had two more visions. I saw both of these visions one day apart when I woke up. The first day I saw a round flat screened television with a white rim about one inch around (this was before flat screens were available). Inside the screen was Robert F. Kennedy showing the upper part of his body. He had on one of those light blue oxford button down shirts that he loved with the sleeves rolled up. Behind on either side of him were buildings. It looked like a college campus. There was a grassy area directly behind him in vivid green and the sky was a beautiful shade of light blue.

I didn't know what the vision meant until I was writing my book *Women of Courage.* Robert F. Kennedy who oversaw the writing of the 1964 Civil Rights Act by his deputy Harold Greene, and his deputy attorney general for civil rights John Doar had inspired me to become a civil rights

156

attorney. I was present in 1963 in the Senate Judiciary Committee Room when he introduced what would become the 1964 Civil Rights Act.

The next day I saw the same vision only this time the man was Father Robert Shanahan, S.J., a friend of my sister's and my mother's and our family. He had died the day before. I knew why I had the vision about Father Shanahan. It was because he wanted me to take care of my mother. These visions were around Thanksgiving that year. At Father's funeral, I told my mother and priest friends of Father Shanahan, including his brother Tom who was also a Jesuit and at Creighton, about my vision of Father Shanahan.

I was so busy working at that time, that I didn't realize until two weeks later that my inner speakings had stopped. I sobbed when I realized this. I don't usually cry but when something hits me I sob. I was so upset that I drove out to Schuyler, Nebraska, to attend one of Father Bill's Masses and healing services. After Mass I got in line for a blessing. When it was my turn, I reminded Father that I was having inner locutions or inner speakings from the Lord. He said: "Yes." He remembered. I said to him: "Father, two weeks ago the inner speakings stopped." I held back the tears. "Will I get them again, or am just to be grateful." Father smiled at me and said: "You are just to be grateful," and he blessed me.

At CSI, I met a co-worker who became my friend until her untimely death in Provo, Utah a few years ago. Her name is Kathryn Studemann. Kathryn had worked at Mutual until she took a buy-out and her pension so she could use the money to educate her two children since their divorced father refused to help them. Kathryn and my mother and I spent many a good Saturday afternoon or Sunday afternoon together going to movies and sharing the expense of Kentucky Fried Chicken, my mother's favorite.

Here I was actively practicing law again when I said I never could. I was still on lithium and other medications, and still seeing one or other psychiatrist every three months and I got emotional strength back. I was ready for the legal battles and life was good again. I named my practice the St. Thomas More Law Center, hoping that one day I would have a team of lawyers to practice innovative non-profit law.

I wrote to the Ford Foundation with a project I wanted funding for called Pro Se, Inc. Pro Se means for yourself. I envisioned a national center to help people all over the country to handle their cases on their own by sending information and forms to them by phone, fax, or mail. I got a nice "no-go" letter from the foundation saying it wasn't in their guidelines.

Many years later Legal Zoom was incorporated by former O.J. Simpson defense attorney Robert Shapiro providing legal assistance to individuals in every state so they can handle their own affairs pro se. They provided the forms and advice how to fill them out. I was ahead of my time and without resources. Legal Zoom uses the internet to obtain clients. It is an online commercial business.

My apartment and law office were on 13th Street near downtown. When I began living there, I was still continuing to have inner speakings. I kept getting the message: "Record, record, record, record." I was afraid to keep a journal because after the Blessed Mother came to Omaha in 1991, I wrote a piece called: "The Story of Another Soul." The story was based on St. Therese's autobiography called *The Story of a Soul.* I told about my inner speakings and some of the messages I got. I sent it to my daughters and my family. Needless to say they regarded it as evidence of delusional thinking. But my daughter Elizabeth bought me Neale Donald's Walsch's *Conversations with God* book for Christmas. This is a book about Mr. Walsch's direct communications with God. He has written several books .Instead of writing everything down after that, I would call my friends and tell them about the messages. Once in 1993, I got a message: "The Pope is coming to Denver." Now I couldn't understand why I got that message. Pope John XXIII was my Pope not particularly Pope John Paul II. I immediately called my friend Joanie Liddell in Denver and told her. She already knew about my messages. There was nothing in the papers about a visit by the Pope to Denver.

About two years later, I saw a picture of Pope John Paul II on the cover of USA Today announcing that the Pope was coming to Denver for International Youth Prayer Day at Cherry Creek Reservoir. I immediately called Joanie and told her that her late husband Dave must be in charge of the selection. I said this because Dave was one of my three close men friends who died in 1982, and I was convinced he was in heaven. Dave had been diagnosed with bi-polar illness that year, and was scheduled to go into a mental hospital. He was so convinced that he would be spending the rest of his life in a mental hospital with no hope of recovery that he bought a gun and went to Cherry Creek Reservoir. Cherry Creek Reservoir is the reservoir that Joanie, Dave and I had taken our kids when my girls and I lived in Denver for a while. It is where he shot himself in the head.

158

In the old days of the Catholic Church, the church denied a Catholic funeral for people who committed suicide, but Dave was given a white vestment Mass, not the black clothed, somber funeral Masses of before. Joanie arranged for a guitar player to play the songs she and Dave loved. It was a beautiful funeral. The wake was held the night before and when we got back to Dave and Joanie's home, the sidewalks in the entire neighborhood were filled with lighted luminaries (brown paper sacks partially filled with sand with lighted candles in them making the sacks transparent lights).

Dave had organized his neighbors years earlier to put the luminaries out every Christmas. And as a tribute to him, they filled the neighborhood sidewalks with these lights. When we drove up the block to their home and witnessed that scene, we all had tears in our eyes.

When I told Joanie that I had purchased USA TODAY and it said the Pope was coming to Denver and that he was going to hold his Mass as Cherry Creek Reservoir, she immediately replied: "Mary Kay, don't you remember that you told me two years ago that the Pope was coming to Denver?" I had completely forgotten. Joanie said she would go to the reservoir to attend the Mass. I told her I would watch it on Mother Angelica's EWTN (Eternal World Television Network) at the same time. All during the Mass, all I could think of was Dave. Years later I learned that Sarah and Dan, the teenage children of my cousin Joe Furay and his wife JoAnn, had been at that Mass too.

While living and working on 13th Street, I had a lawyer I was up against file a complaint against me with the Nebraska Bar Association Counsel on Discipline because I used the name St. Thomas More Law Center for my practice. He said I didn't have permission from St. Thomas More to use his name. Dennis Carlson, the counsel on discipline wrote and asked me to respond. I wrote back that while I didn't have St. Thomas More's permission to use his name, I had asked his boss for permission and he said "yes." The complaint was dismissed and I was allowed to continue to use St. Thomas More's name. St. Thomas More, the patron saint of lawyers, was the lawyer saint who was beheaded by King Henry VIII in England because St. Thomas opposed the King's divorce and his separation of England from the Catholic Faith. There was a movie about St. Thomas More called *A Man for All Seasons.*

Sundance and Cherokee Moon

In the beginning I told you about my passion for movies. Even after I returned to Omaha from Cherokee when my Social Security checks started coming, I went to the movies just about every Saturday. Sometimes I would go alone, sometimes I would go with Elizabeth when she got a break from her law studies, sometimes I would go with my friend Shirley Dean whom I met in 1966 when we were both Douglas County Assistance Bureau caseworkers, sometimes with Kathryn Studemann and/ or my mother and Kathryn.

One time Shirley and Kathryn and I went to see *Girl Interrupted* a movie with Angelina Jolie (she played a rather sadistic patient and won a best supporting actress Academy Award). The movie, which also had Whoopi Goldberg playing a psychiatric nurse, took place in a mental hospital and was the story of four young women. Both Shirley and Kathryn asked me afterward if the movie was like my experiences at Cherokee and St. Joe's. The movie showed the use of restraints, or tying people down. I told them that I had never seen restraints in my two stays but that the bonding between the patients with each other was true. There is a tremendous bonding among patients.

It was when I was living on 13th Street that I developed dizziness and numbness of both feet. I had a severe attack of dizziness on the elevator in the Douglas County District Courthouse when another lawyer was with me. After questioning me about all my symptoms including unquenchable thirst, he told me he thought I was diabetic. "I'm diabetic," he told me.

I was receiving my medical care at the University of Nebraska Medical Center. After blood tests, my doctor confirmed that I was a type II diabetic. Now diabetes is a common side effect of psychiatric medications which cause excessive weight gain, and some of those medications actually cause diabetes, and I had a predisposition toward it because my Grandmother Bess Phelan was a type I or juvenile diabetic. I was given medication and a blood sugar monitor and entered into a weight loss program.

Needless to say, I didn't like being a diabetic, although the discipline necessary regarding food management and blood sugar control and exercise can make you healthier than non-diabetics. My grandmother Bess Phelan had lost the lower part of one leg to the disease, and couldn't learn to walk without crutches because the leg she lost was her good leg.

160

Sundance and Cherokee Moon

I moved from 13th Street to an apartment in the Dundee area on 48th Street. I still lived there in 2000, the year of the Millennium. As I mentioned before, I saw in a Newsweek Magazine that Pope John Paul II had named St. Therese, the Little Flower of Jesus, and the saint for the Millennium. And the article noted that her relics and a photo display of her life were being sent around the world. And the article gave the cities and dates of that display in the United States. The closest city to Omaha was Sioux City, Iowa. I asked my mother if she wanted to go with me up to Sioux City. She was excited to go. We stood in line with 6,000 people the paper reported. We saw people we knew from Omaha. There was a reverential silence in the crowd as we approached one by one to the reliquary, or beautiful, large wooden box containing her relics.

Like I noted earlier, we were given laminated prayer cards with her picture on them and told to touch the prayer cards to the reliquary and that the cards would thus be relics themselves. We took enough cards for everyone in the family especially for my sister Therese who was named after St. Therese. Next we were led into a room with mounted photographs of St. Therese and her family before she entered the convent, pictures of her home, of the convent and of her in her Carmelite habit. She and her own sisters had entered the Carmelite convent. My mother and I were both thrilled with this experience.

The reason Sioux City had been chosen was because there is a Carmelite convent in Sioux City. When I got home, I called the convent and thanked the sister on the phone for sharing this exhibit with us. I told her about my trip to Des Moines in 1988 and the vision I had with Jesus on the Cross, the Blessed Mother on my right facing Jesus and St. Therese on the left facing me and that I had asked St. Therese what she was doing there. The sister said that I was blessed to have had that vision. Before I hung up, I asked the sister her name. She replied: "I am Mother Therese."

I developed stomach problems about this time. I started vomiting frequently for no known cause. The vomiting became almost constant. It eventually was so severe that I couldn't work anymore. I went to Dr. Michael Sorrell, M.D., a gastroenterologist at the University of Nebraska Medical Center (recently they named the Nebraska University Medical School the Michael Sorrell School of Medicine). Dr. Sorrell ran a series of tests and discovered that half of the staples were no longer in my stomach. He urged me to have surgery to reverse the stomach stapling surgery. I resisted because I have such a low pain threshold and the original surgery had cause me so much pain. But the vomiting caused me another problem, I could not hold down all my psychiatric and diabetes medications. I was spending a week at a time either in the emergency room getting IV's or a week at a time in the University of Nebraska Medical Center Clarkson Hospital getting IV's and taking my meds.

I was on Medicaid for my meds, and they would only allow one month of pills for each prescription. This fact and my constant vomiting and not being able to hold down my meds resulted in causing me to suffer a slow mania that resulted in a severe episode of mania and delusions.

CHAPTER 14: THREE MENTAL HOSPITALS IN FOUR WEEKS

Late 1989 or 1990, I panicked about the prospect of gaining more weight from Lithium, so I had stomach stapling surgery. I never lost the weight people are supposed to lose from the surgery. And my recovery was extremely painful due to that low pain threshold. Several years later, after I was diagnosed with Type II Diabetes in 1995, I went through a weight loss program at the University of Nebraska Medical Center under the supervision of my primary doctor Robert Bowman, M.D. and managed to lose 50 lbs and my Diabetes went into remission.

Diabetes is a serious health condition that can cause amputation of the feet and legs, heart disease and blindness among other things. It has become the dangerous condition of young people today because of the high fructose corn syrup in all the processed foods and fast foods we eat. It is a national epidemic. Many doctors now claim that sugar and high fructose corn syrup, a corn sugar product, are toxic and can cause all forms of disease including diabetes and brain problems and cancer. First Lady Michele Obama has been fighting for the exclusion of these foods in the school lunch program promoting healthy food for America's kid's meals.

Finally during one of my hospitalizations, a nurse recommended I go to a gastroenterologist or stomach doctor. I was very lucky to get Dr. Michael Sorrell, M.D. as my doctor. After a series of tests, he found out that only half of the stomach staples were still in place. This had something to do with all my vomiting. He recommended surgery. As I previously noted, I was afraid to have the surgery to remove all the staples because of the extreme pain I suffered with the original surgery. I resisted the surgery.

One time after not being able to keep my medications down, I became manic or extremely high. I was living in an apartment at the time. I was in a happy manic state to begin with. Once I walked over to my mother's apartment and before getting there, I stopped at a music store and they let me play the piano. I was playing the piano and singing until a customer came in. The staff very kindly asked me if I would go because they wanted to help this customer. I went up to my mother's and she noted how high I was and asked me if I would be willing to go to Immanuel Hospital. My younger brother drove mother and me to the emergency room. The doctor agreed that I should be hospitalized for my mania and asked me if I would voluntarily accept hospitalization. I agreed. I was sent to the mental ward that evening.

When I awoke the next morning and got dressed, I noted that the blanket in my room looked just like the saris or clothing of Mother's Teresa's order. The blanket had light blue wide stripes at the top and the bottom of the white blanket. I put the blanket on my head and wrapped it around me. I looked in the mirror. I looked just like one of Mother Teresa's sisters.

(When Helen, my mother and I regularly went to Father Halley's Legion of Mary group, one of our members named Michael had served five years working with Mother Teresa. A book about Mother Teresa came out during this time with lots of pictures. I spotted Michael in one of the pictures. The men wore clothing with the same wide blue stripes on their white clothing as did the sisters. Helen and I went in together and bought the expensive book for Michael. Michael was in medical school during our days with Father Halley. He graduated, did his residency and happily married and had a number of children.)

Back at Immanuel Mental Health Center, there were no windows in the room where I slept. When I walked down the hallway, I came upon a long, narrow window and stopped. I could see the Miracle of the Sun. I started praying seeing the Miracle of the Sun like I always do, and all of a sudden a rather large nurse yelled at me that I needed to go to another room because the doctor would be seeing patients there. I wanted to continue praying for a while so I told her: "Let the doctor know that I am here."

All of a sudden I was surrounded by six men in black uniforms who shoved me into another ward, a locked ward, and shoved me into a locked room with a metal bed and no mattress and flung me up in the air and dropped me down face down onto the metal bed. My face was shoved into a pillow. I lifted my head and screamed: "Get that pillow away from me, I am suffocating." The pillow was pulled to the floor and I suddenly felt a sharp pain in my hip. I was injected with something and immediately went out.

Six hours later, I came to and noticed the door was now open. I got up and moving slowly walked into the main room where the patients were sitting. They greeted me and asked me if I was okay. I asked them what happened to me. They told me that I was probably given a shot of Haldol, an anti-psychotic medication. They informed me that I was in the locked ward. I knew one of the young men from my mother's building. He was a great guy. He told me his story during my stay.

There was nothing to do in that room but sit in chairs and to talk to each other. There was no television or radio, there were no books or magazines; we were basically warehoused in confinement. There were no windows in the room. The only windows were in the bedrooms and we were only allowed in our rooms to share a bathroom with the next room and to sleep. The bedrooms were locked. We had to find a nurse if we needed to go to the bathroom. This was almost a disaster for me. We had no natural light during sixteen hours a day.

We had metal tables without cloths to eat on. After being there a few days, I organized my fellow patients to decorate our table. We spread our napkins out to make a table cloth and we put all our straws together in a glass to make a bouquet. It was not the French Café in the Old Market, but it was an improvement over the sterile mental table tops.

I was complaining about our conditions when a nurse said to me: "You are here voluntarily. You can leave whenever you want." So I got my purse and went downstairs to the main hospital and called a cab and went home. The glass door in my apartment was broken out. I think I called the police to report it. I slept there anyway. The landlord fixed the door the next day. A few days after that, I became delusional. I took most of my clothes out of the closet and placed them all outdoors on a table outside my door. I'd like to be able to tell you that I was acting like St. Francis who gave all his clothes away to the poor, but that was not my state of mind. I did give them away to low income people, but I had lost some weight and believed I had money coming to buy a new wardrobe.

I no longer had a car. It had died on the highway. It was towed. When I was contacted by the towing company, the charge for the tow and storage far exceeded what income I had at the time. But this day, the day of giving my clothes away, I walked down the hill to a car lot. I knew the owner slightly through Mary Cornett, and told her I wanted to buy a car. She gave me a car I selected and told me to take it out to go to the bank and get my money to buy the car. I was deluded thinking that I had money.

I drove that car for miles until I decided to take the car to Kansas City to show my daughters my new car. I sincerely thought I had bought the car by this time. I ran out of gas on highway I-29 on the Iowa side. A

Sundance and Cherokee Moon

highway patrolman stopped me and came to my window. I gave him all my information and my driver's license. He asked me if I was related to Professor Pat Green at Creighton University Law School. It turned out that this patrolman was a student of my brother's. He left and another patrolman had someone from a gas station put a gallon of gas in the tank to get me to his station ahead.

But the driver in his truck did not signal a turn and I missed the turnoff. I eventually ran out of gas again and the second patrolman came and made me get out of the car and into the patrol car. He asked me why I didn't turn into the station and where I was going. He had his partner drive the car and they took me back to their patrol station where they made me wait.

Eventually my brothers came with a woman I didn't know. The first patrolman had called my brother Pat. I had told the second patrolman that I was going to make a movie and this incident would be in it. I even asked him who he wanted to play him. A few years earlier, I told one of my classmates that they were going to make a movie of the screenplay I wrote "They Let Mothers in Law School?" I was in the first large class of women at Creighton University Law School and one of several mothers. We were in the first class at Creighton Law School with mother students.

My brothers told me that I hadn't bought the car, and the lot owner knowing one of them had called my brother rather than the police. I was taken to Mercy Hospital in Council Bluffs where I was hospitalized. I was in an open ward and still a bit ditzy or manic. One of the younger women and I started talking. She was a young mother with a child and living with her boyfriend. I asked her if they ever held themselves out as married, and she said yes. I told her that Iowa recognized common law marriage and that she was married.

I want to interject that last year, I was having lunch with four of my ex-nun friends from Mercy High School and the Sisters of Mercy in Omaha. Joanie Sheehan, Sr. Judy Healey, JoAnn Shannon and Michaele Ann or "Mike" Pleiss (she took the traditional route and married a wonderful man and they have seven children). (Sixteen of us from my high school class went into the Sisters of Mercy together. Seven of us have stayed together over the years). Lynn Beutel, Rosemary King and I live away from Omaha. Of the rest, Sr. Judy, Joanie, Mike and JoAnn and I try to get together for lunch at the Brazenhead Irish Pub in Omaha whenever I come up to Omaha. While Mike took the traditional route and got married and

166

had seven children. Lynn, Rose and JoAnn entered into traditional marriages after they left the convent. JoAnn had to leave the convent for health reasons. She married and has a son. Lynn and Rose married too and have children. Mike, Lynn, Rose, JoAnn and I all have children and grandchildren.

Well at lunch, I was talking to them about this book and I told them there was one story I wasn't going to include in the book because it was too painful. I told them the story about the car. Well to my surprise they all started laughing. I couldn't believe it. This story was so humiliating to me. But they explained that there had been a series of ads for a car company where the people took the cars out to test them and kept them all day and night going out to eat and to the movies, etc. They insisted that I keep the car story in the book.

Well back at Mercy Hospital, the next day, a tall, substantial, uniformed security guard came up to me and asked me to go with him. I followed him into another ward. He told me that I had to stay there. It was the locked ward, and I was the only patient in there. There was a glassed-in nursing station, but the only human contact I had was for 15 minutes a day when a woman psychiatrist came to talk to me. I was still not able to hold down my medicines.

The ward had a main room, shower rooms, toilets and single bedrooms with the same metal beds they had at Immanuel except there were five inch thick mattresses on the beds. I did not do well in solitary confinement. I had no stimulation or conversation. To keep my mind sane, I took the mattress off my bed and danced on the metal bed and sang every song that I had ever heard. I did this for a few days. Then I was taken downstairs one morning to a room. My mother and my older brother were in the room.

A man who identified himself as an administrative law judge sat at the end of the table directly opposite to me. On my left was a former law classmate. I was told by the judge that my classmate was there as my lawyer, but he never spoke to me. I guess Iowa was like Nebraska where your attorney doesn't have to talk to you. At some level I knew what was going on but I couldn't deal with it. I had gotten used to playing the piano with my fingers for years while hearing the music in my head. I did this throughout the hearing and did not respond to any questions by the judge.

Sundance and Cherokee Moon

The next thing I knew, I was in a car being driven somewhere. I deluded myself into thinking that I was being taken somewhere to meet President Bill Clinton, but in a couple of hours when the car turned left into a driveway, I saw that old familiar sign: "Cherokee State Mental Hospital." I was committed to the locked ward, the dreaded locked ward.

Unlike the locked wards at Immanuel and Mercy, the locked ward at Cherokee was a large central ward with a piano off to the side. There were games, paper, pens and colors, large windows to look out of, multiply bed bedrooms, a dining room, large bathrooms and showers and lots of patients to talk to. I was still vomiting, but eventually I would be able to hold down enough food and medicine that in two weeks I was released.

One evening, I heard someone screaming. I followed the screams down the hall until I got to the door where the screams were coming from. I opened the door to see if I could help. Two staff members were trying to pull a heavy set patient up into bed by grabbing her up by her hands and hurting her. One of them demanded that I shut the door and go away. Like a good mother, I told them: "I won't leave until you stop hurting her." I was immediately surrounded by numerous staff who tried to force me back away from the room. Having just come from the violence on me at Immanuel, I tried to prevent the same thing from happening again. I put my right leg out and turned around and around in a circle on my left leg, but I got extremely tired and could not hold my right leg up anymore.

Then it happened, the crowd of staff got ahold of me and forced me into a locked room where they lifted me up on a high table-like fixture. They immediately strapped down my legs, spread my arms out onto a cross board and strapped my arms down too. I look down at my arms and legs and my outstretched body and I thought: "This is the new crucifixion, the crucifixion of people with mental illness." For the first time I was kept in restraints. It was the last time too.

There was no way that I was going to let them inject me with Haldol again so I began to sing every song I ever heard like I did at Mercy Hospital and I sang all night until seven o'clock in the morning. At that shift change, a nurse came in and gently said that if I agreed to take my medicine, she would remove all the restraints and I would be free to leave the room. I agreed.

Sundance and Cherokee Moon

Well I had gotten to know one young man because we both regularly played the piano. I left the room and went out and sat down on a couch where he was sitting. He said: "I enjoyed your singing last night." "You could hear everything?" I asked. "Yes, I was in the room next to you. I especially liked your song about insurrection." "Insurrection!" I asked: "I sang a song about insurrection?" "Yes," he replied, "That was my favorite song." I realized then that when I ran out of songs, I started creating them myself. "Insurrection," I thought, "that must have been the Irish rebel in me."

I showed my creativity again in the locked unit. I went to the big table and got some paper and colored pens. I started the next few days drawing caricatures or drawings of people's faces. The patients whose faces I drew liked the drawings so much that they asked me if they could keep them. Other patients came up to me over the days to have me draw their faces. Even the nurses asked me to draw their faces. I did a character drawing of my own face too. I still have that drawing in a slim black briefcase along with the automatic writing I experienced in Chicago on the way home from Medjugorje. The briefcase is buried in all my stuff over in Mary Kay's basement.

There are two other incidents I want to share with you. First, there was a young woman there at Cherokee in the locked ward who didn't speak. I didn't know if she was mute or if there was some other reason she didn't speak. But she understood everything she heard. She motioned to me that she wanted me to draw her face, too. I did, and while I was drawing her face, I talked to her. I asked her if she would like me to write a letter to her family for her. She nodded "yes." I would say something and ask her if that was what she wanted to say and she would shake her head "Yes." When the letter was done, I gave it to her and told her to have the staff mail her letter to her family. She wanted to see her family. She was a very sweet young woman.

The next incident involved the women's restroom. The toilet stalls were at the far end of the room. There was a long wall mirror in the room when you first came in, with a ledge to put your things on below the mirror. Several of us were standing looking into the mirror and looking at each other. One of the women facing the mirror started speaking. She was a brilliant woman. This time she said: "If Jesus comes again, he will be a woman!" We all shook our heads: "Yes." That was about the most religion we got on the locked ward, but I still said my private prayers for my fellow patients and my girls and my family and friends.

This might be a good place to add that a few years later Rosie O'Donnell started her daytime television show. I loved her comedy but I also loved the fact that she could sing every song she ever heard just like I could at Mercy Hospital and Cherokee.

At the end of the two weeks, a nurse told me to get my things together because I would be going home. A very nice woman came up to the ward to get me. We went downstairs and out to a waiting car. The driver was a man. He was nice too. They talked to me the whole ride into Omaha. I directed them to my mother's apartment. I got out of the car the same time as the woman and she came over and hugged me.

The last time I left Cherokee, I got a hug too. That time it was from a fellow patient. We had ridden the bus together to go home. By the way, my mother was home and glad to see me. I lived in her apartment with her for two years until I went to Kansas City. It was a one bedroom apartment and I slept on the floor on a sleeping bag. Every Sunday my sister Liz and her girls took us to Mass and out to breakfast. On Saturdays we went to the movies.

I wasn't home a week yet when I went into a depression. I was afraid to have the stomach stapling surgery reversed fearful of the pain involved, and I couldn't live that way with vomiting and hospitalizations anymore. I told the Lord that I could not go into one more mental hospital. I was torn between the surgery and suicide. I opted for the surgery after Dr. Sorrell also told me: "Mary Kay, you can't live this way."

Both Dr. Sorrell and the surgeon Dr. Johnson warned me that the diabetes might come back. I had the surgery in November, 2002. Not knowing that the diabetes had come back right away, I ate sugar products and the diabetes and weight gain came back in a year. The good news is that I have not vomited once since the surgery in November, 2002 and I lost the weight again.

My lifelong friend Shirley Dean took me into her home after I was released from the hospital after the surgery. She let me stay there for a month. That was how long I suffered with the pain. Shirley, my other Lutheran friend along with Carole Barnes, participated in every Sacrament of the Catholic

Sundance and Cherokee Moon

Church except confession and Holy Orders. She was present when a priest from the Cathedral Parish came to the hospital and gave me the Sacrament of Healing. I had no memory of that since I was on heavy doses of morphine. I had the Sacrament of Healing at St. Margaret Mary's Church from one of the priests there before the surgery. I was doubly annointed.

Shirley died a few years ago after a long illness with cancer. I lost so many friends to cancer. She had smoked as a young woman but she quit smoking thirty years before she died. Cancer didn't care. She had so many friends from all her work in the field of working with people with retardation or intellectual impairment. She had many friends who were disabled and helped them to have normal lives. She was close to her family, none of whom lived in Omaha. She was much loved by everyone.

A couple of years before she died, she introduced me to her friend and new neighbor Patty McGill Smith who became my close friend too. I knew Patty's brother, Judge Michael McGill from college at Creighton. One year he was elected as president of the student board of governors and I was elected secretary of the board. He dated Jane Bernica, a close friend of mine at the time too until she went into the convent. Years after she left the convent she married a fellow Creighton grad Walt Mullaney and had a family. She died in her thirties of cancer. Jane was like a sister to me.

Patty, the mother of seven whose youngest daughter is autistic and challenged and a wonderful, loving human being, had just returned to Omaha after being Under Secretary of Education in Washington, D.C. under President Ronald Reagan and George H.W. Bush and the reason she was appointed was because she developed a program for parents to help them help their disabled children.

An article she wrote titled "You Are Not Alone" has been published in several languages, with millions of copies distributed. It is still on the internet republished if you enter Patricia McGill Smith in your search engine. Author William Bennett included the entire article in a book he wrote. Patty has traveled all over the world working with parents and others to establish this parent program. Patty, a brilliant woman and terrific mother rose all the way up to the top of government service appointed by two Presidents only with a high school diploma. When she graduated from high school, her parents would not let her take a scholarship she had from Creighton. Girls were to be married. Boys were to be educated. In her career, she surpassed all her brothers who got to go

171

to college and two who became lawyers with her appointment as undersecretary.

I went to Kansas City in January of 2003 to dog sit for my daughter Elizabeth's dogs when she attended a workshop in Washington, D.C. She was working for the Navy in Belton, MO near Kansas City as a civilian contract specialist. She was seriously injured in a car accident there and was barely able to fly home. I took care of her after two surgeries and for rehab for six months until she was able to go back to work. At the end of the six months, my grandson Michael asked me to move to Kansas City which I did at his request.

The only other hospital I was ever in after Cherokee and moving to Kansas City was at Two Rivers Hospital in a day program for two weeks while my Geodon dosage, my new medicine, was increased and took effect. The program was excellent. It was two weeks of intensive group therapy, role playing and discussions. The hospital had a driver, a great guy named Michael and a van. I was the first one Michael picked up in the morning since I lived the farthest away. He picked up all the patients. We got to be friends and he would bring special music CD's to play for me each day. Michael had taken the job after Sprint Cellphone Company fired most of their senior employees. There was a big class action age discrimination case filed against Sprint and Michael was one of several plaintiffs. It took a long time, but the case finally settled. I ran into Michael once at the symphony. It was good to see him.

I have been on Geodon and Lamictal since 2004 and I have not been hospitalized since Two Rivers and I have had no side effects. These two drugs gave me back my life. Two Rivers was my favorite hospital because of the program and that it was only during the day. St. Joseph was good after I got out of the locked ward, and so was Richard Young where I voluntarily admitted myself to get off of Depakote. But the best inpatient hospital was Cherokee the first time with all that freedom and in the locked ward with all those windows and so much you could do. Subtracting that horrific incident with the restraints, the facility at Cherokee was the best. There is a national movement to eliminate and/or limit the use of restraints. I have offered my testimony before about this.

If anyone is going to build a new mental hospital, I would be an excellent advisor both regarding the program and regarding the building. I have already had my on the job training. In addition, I am a lawyer. Contact me at mkgkansascity17@gmail.com. I am serious.

CHAPTER 15: THREE PRO SE LAWSUITS

I filed three pro se (in Latin meaning "for yourself") lawsuits representing myself. The first lawsuit was captioned Mary Kay Green v. Governor Robert Ray, U.S. District Court for Iowa at Council Bluffs. I filed this lawsuit to record the conditions at Cherokee after the head doctor for the women's ward asked me to contact former U.S. Senator Harold E. Hughes for help. Among other things, they did not have enough money for therapists or mattresses. I wasn't able to get back in touch with Senator Hughes as the head doctor asked me to, so I did the next best thing; I went to court.

I lost this lawsuit in court but after the lawsuit, Governor Ray graciously invited me to be on his special mental health committee in Des Moines. We had a major snowstorm for the first meeting so I missed it and I didn't have the money to travel every month to Iowa after that so I wasn't able to accept. I also contacted my friend Iowa State senator Mike Gronstal about the need for more funding at Cherokee. He told me that there was a move to close it. I said that would be wrong. I checked into the status of Cherokee recently and it has become a mental health center.

The second lawsuit I filed in 1995 is now captioned <u>Mary Kay Green</u> v. <u>James Jansen, County Attorney, Tom Kenney, Public Defender</u> in the U.S. District Court for Nebraska at Omaha challenging the Constitutionality of the Nebraska Mental Health Commitment Law.

The original caption for the case was captioned Mary Kay Green v Judge Elizabeth Crnkovich (my sister) et al including other family members and Jansen and Kenney. I was encouraged to file this lawsuit by my psychiatrist Dr. Glenda Housel, M.D. after I questioned with her the right of my family to keep trying to commit me. When Dr. Housel learned that I was a lawyer, she told me I had to use my law degree to help other people with mental illness. She suggested I challenge the Constitutionality of the Nebraska Mental Health Commitment Law.

I went regularly to the Creighton University Law School Library. I found the law library subscribed to the American Bar Association *Mental Health Law Reporter*. This reporter discussed the various laws in the 50 states and the court decisions. Through the Law Reporter, I found a Creighton

Sundance and Cherokee Moon

Law Review article documenting why the State Mental Health Commitment law was unconstitutional.

The States were divided on committing people with mental illness. Most states provided a hearing before a judge in open court. Iowa and Nebraska provided for administrative hearings. In Iowa the hearing is before an administrative law judge. In Nebraska they have mental health commitment boards comprised of lawyers, lay people, and the Clerk of the District Court. In Missouri, psychiatrists are the ones who file commitment proceedings.

Dr.Housel told me to list my younger, number seven child, sister Liz, Judge Elizabeth Crnkovich, first because we would get publicity for the challenge of the law then. We did. It was painful for me to do this. *The Omaha World Herald* reporter interviewed me and the paper ran a prominent article.

About this time, Dr. Housel told me she was taking a job at the University of Maryland Medical School and that the psychiatrists there were very progressive and that she could get me a lot of help in changing the law. I tried to write her later when she went into private practice. At no time did she or her group provide any assistance. I was out there alone.

In the meantime after I filed the lawsuit, I contacted the lawyer who wrote the law review article when she was clerking for a federal judge. Actually, I contacted that judge, Judge Urbom, and asked him to let her know that I had filed the lawsuit based on her law review article. She wrote back. She didn't say "great" or "good luck." Her only concern was that people should know that she was not behind the lawsuit. Well, it is true that I was not in contact with her personally, but she did write the law review article. Wasn't it her goal that someone would use it to challenge the statute? She was practicing law in Minnesota at the time. I threw her letter away and never wrote back.

Armed with the law review article and the cases I found in the Mental Health Law Reporter, I was able to defeat the Motions of the Public Defender and the County Attorney for Summary Judgment so the judge's decision in my favor was the law. The judge also wrote in his decision that I should go to the Supreme Court to get a decision finding the law unconstitutional. I had moved out of state after that and did not pursue the Nebraska Supreme Court case.

After I filed the lawsuit, my law professor brother Pat called me and met with me and asked me what I wanted to achieve with the lawsuit. I told him that I wanted the statute to be declared unconstitutional. He said: "If that's what you want then drop everyone from the case except the County Attorney and the Public Defender. I did this. The County Attorney and the Public Defender both filed Motions for Summary Judgment. The Public Defender hired one of the big law firms to represent him. The County Attorney used his own staff. They both lost. That law review article and I prevailed.

I had moved to Kansas with Mary Kay. It was after I came back to Omaha from Kansas that I contacted Dr. Glenda Housel, M.D. She had been one of the psychiatrists I saw at Douglas County Hospital and she was now in private practice. My hospitalization in St. Joseph's Hospital by my family was the basis of my action in federal court.

Another lawsuit I filed was <u>Mary Kay Green</u> v <u>Jack Wisman, M.D., and Joseph Stankus, Ph.D.</u> in the Douglas County District Court. The case was transferred to Sarpy County so Judge Ronald Reagan was the judge. After a hearing, Judge Reagan said from the bench that I sued the wrong people that I should have sued the County Attorney's office. He dismissed the case against the doctors. I had difficulty deposing my sister Liz during discovery. Judge Reagan had to supervise the entire deposition. I asked my sister if she was afraid of me and she replied yes. I was not a violent person. I was shocked by her answer.

A year or so later I had a case in Juvenile Court in Omaha. I was waiting in the lobby of the Juvenile Court until my case was called. It was before another judge. Liz walked in and saw me and came over and sat next to me and took my hand. "How are you?" she asked. We both had tears in our eyes. This was the moment of our reconciliation. I wrote Judge Reagan to tell him about our reunion.

I must add that my two brothers and my sister Liz's actions were another example of God's protection of me. I had no place to stay in Des Moines, I didn't know how I would get back, and I later learned that the Senator was in Arizona at the time, so their decision to stop me was a good decision made out of love, which I can say in retrospect. From their perspective, I had once fled from them in Iowa. I wouldn't have fled after my brothers came to Steven's Center to get me, but how were they to know.

During discovery of this case, I took psychologist Dr. Joseph Stankus' deposition. It became clear from his answers to my questions that he believed in my spiritual experiences. I asked him why he didn't try to help me. He answered that I wasn't his patient that I was Dr. Wisman's patient. I only had enough money to take Dr. Stankus' deposition. I could not afford to take Dr. Wiseman's deposition. Dr. Stankus's deposition supported my spiritual experiences and was favorable to me and I thought it would be.

During my sessions with him, I told him about being asked to join the Poor Clare Sisters and about Father Bill's healing services. He asked me to have Father pray for him. He had a major decision to make in his life. I liked both Dr. Stankus and Dr. Wisman and still do. I just lost trust in Dr. Wisman and I wanted to find out what had happened. This was back when you didn't have a right to your own medical records.

CHAPTER 16: THE BLESSED MOTHER AT CARITAS, ALABAMA

Helen called me one day in late 2010. She had received a booklet in the mail about the coming apparitions of the Blessed Mother in the community of Caritas near Birmingham, Alabama. The visionary Marija Lunneti from Medjugorje was going to be there in March of 2011. For five days starting March 19, 2011, the Blessed Mother would be appearing to Marija and people were urged to come to be present during those apparitions. Helen sent me the booklet.

Marija had been coming to Caritas regularly about every two years since the time she and her brother came there so she could donate one of her kidneys to him in 1988. I had heard about her visits years before when I read *Medjugorje Magazine* published by Caritas. I subscribed to that magazine until they stopped publishing it. This time was right for me to go. I had enough money to pay for the plane fare and I got an inexpensive rate for a motel. I rented a car at the airport for the five days. It was not expensive. I got in to my motel the night before the first apparition.

The next morning I drove some miles to find Caritas. I couldn't find it at first and had to stop to get instructions about where to turn off the highway. There was no sign saying "Caritas." I got there about 10:00 a.m. People were in the field where the apparitions took place three of the five days. They were saying the rosary. The other two apparitions would take place in the home of the director and his wife in their bedroom.

One of the Franciscan priests from Medjugorje had given the director (who prefers to be called "A Friend of Medjugorje" in all his writings), the crucifix from his room in St. James Church in Medjugorje where the Blessed Mother appeared to the visionaries when he was protecting them while Father Jozo was in jail. Father was being reassigned to another city and knew of the work at Caritas where all the Blessed Mother's messages are printed. In 2011, they were both printed and sent over the internet at www.Mej.com or www.Medjugorje.com.

That first morning after I said the rosary with the crowd of people, we surrounded the statue of the Blessed Mother and the large oak tree nearby where the Blessed Mother had been appearing to Marija during her earlier visits. After praying with everyone, I went back to the road and walked up the hill to the top where the building housing a chapel and two floors of production were located. Those two floors were for the printing and distribution of the Blessed Mother's messages in book form annually updated. The books are titled *Words from Heaven.* These books and other religious items can be purchased in person at the Medjugorje Book Store there or by phone (205-672-2000) or at Medjugorje.com or Mej.com. Information about Caritas can be obtained from a search engine putting "Caritas of Birmingham."

That first time up the hill, I had to stop twice to get my breath. The last three days I zipped up that hill. When I stopped halfway up a very nice woman from Maryland stopped to talk to me. She had learned about the time of the apparition that first day and shared that information with me. She also told me about the buildings at the top and where the eating area and portable toilets were. I ran into her again and that evening I joined her and her son in the field to watch Marija transfixed during Our Lady's apparition to her. Afterward, Marija took a microphone and announced what Our Lady said to her and that Our Lady blessed us and all the religious items we had with us. Her talk about Our Lady's message was recorded then and printed later and sent by email throughout the world and distributed to us the next day.

During each apparition, Our Lady would tell the time and the place of her next apparition. As I indicated, three times the apparitions were in the field. Twice they were in the director and his wife's bedroom where the crucifix from Medjugorje hung over the bed. These two times, Marija would come from the home to the field where she would announce Our Lady's messages and the times of the next apparition. Again Our Lady's messages for those days were always printed and sent by the internet all over the world.

One day my friend from Maryland and her son took me up to Irondale, Alabama, where Mother Angelica first started her Eternal World Television Network and where it is still broadcast from there to date. We got to go into the building housing the studio and see where the shows were produced. In a separate building was the chapel where the Mass was broadcast from each day. There was also a very large religious book store next door. Mother Angelica had built a new church and convent about thirty miles from Irondale. You can see the sisters and Mother Angelica in the new church during their broadcasts of the rosary. But when Mother and the sisters lived in Irondale, you could see them in the back of the altar during Mass and when they came forward for Communion during Mass.

For the last two days before I left, we could go into the director's home ten at a time and we could kneel and pray in the bedroom in front of the crucifix from Medjugorje. We were given sheets of paper to write the names of all the people we were praying for and for our intentions. We were told to place them on the bed as the Blessed Mother had told the people in the Caritas community to do before. This room was a holy place and not a sound was made as we all prayed. I got to stand in line and pray in the bedroom two days.

The last evening that the Blessed Mother appeared to Marija in the field, Marija was kneeling in front of the statue of the Blessed Mother near the large oak tree and talking to the "Friend of Medjugorje." The statue of Mary (see the picture I took of it after the apparition) was surrounded by bouquets of roses, and around the roses were five rows of lit candles in a circle. I was standing just opposite Marija on the other side of the ring of candles. All of a sudden she turned her head and folded her hands and looked up to where the Blessed Mother was appearing. The apparition was taking place. I was close enough that I could see her lips moving as she talked with the Blessed Mother.

When the Blessed Mother left to go back to heaven, Marija stood and went to the microphone and announced to all of us the message the Blessed Mother gave to her for us and noted that the Blessed Mother blessed each of us and all our religious items. As Marija was leaving to go across the field and back to the director's home where she was staying, she greeted everyone on either side of her. I was able to get over to her side and shake hands with her and thank her for coming. I was filled with such joy that evening.

In 1988, Ivan's apparitions were way up in the choir loft. We could see him immediately kneel down when the Blessed Mother came but no one was around him to actually see him talking to the Blessed Mother. I was very blessed to witness Marija talking to the Blessed Mother. Marija had spent one afternoon in the area up on top of the hill talking to people and answering their questions. This was the afternoon that my friends from Maryland and I went up to Irondale to EWTN and Mother Angelica's chapel and buildings so we missed this opportunity to talk to her. This event was unscheduled.

180

One other family I got close to at Caritas was a family from New England. They were a mother, her adult son and her granddaughter. The grandmother confessed to me that they came for spiritual and emotional healings. The son and his wife had separated and this caused deep depression in their daughter. Because of this, the son and his wife were trying to reconcile. I told the grandmother my story living with mental illness and told her that I had been praying for her granddaughter for years. She asked me how that could be when I only met her there. I explained that every day for years, I have prayed for people suffering from mental illness along with my other daily prayers. I asked her to tell her granddaughter my story and that I would continue to pray for her.

I came home with many blessed religious items to give to family and friends including a baby blanket blessed by the Blessed Mother for my nephew and his wife's expected baby. Since Erik and Julie were waiting to be surprised about the sex of their baby, I had the blanket inscribed as "Blessed by the Blessed Mother at Caritas for Baby Wright." The baby was a girl. They subsequently had another girl and the blanket could be used for her too.

Returning from Caritas, I gave almost everything I bought away, but I still have a statue of the Blessed Mother blessed by her on my book shelf. And Grace Ann Ancona brought me back a rosary blessed by the Blessed Mother when she first went to Medjugorje three years ago. The next year Grace Ann and her husband Frank went together. He was just as moved as she was. In June, 2014 Grace Ann and a friend went to Lourdes, Liseaux and Medjugorje by themselves. They were met in Paris with a guide arranged by a woman living in Lees Summit who was originally from the Medjugorje area.

CHAPTER 17: FATHER WHELAN IS A BEACON AND A LIGHT TO HEAL THE NATION

When Father Bill Whelan was still at St. Margaret Mary's Parish in Omaha, one time my daughter Elizabeth accompanied my mother and me to his weekly healing service. This was the only time that she accompanied us. We joined Helen in the church. While Father Whelan was giving his healing talk, I heard a loud voice say: "Father Whelan is a beacon and a light to heal the nation and you are to bear witness to this."

I assumed that everyone in the Church heard this loud voice, but after everything was over, I asked Elizabeth, my mother and Helen if they had heard it too. They each said "yes." We asked others too. No one else but the four of us heard God's voice.

Later, Helen and I told Father about this incidence and we asked him if he knew what it meant. He said he didn't know but that he would be in prayer about it.

This book and everything in it about Father Whelan is the fulfillment of my obligation given to me by God to bear witness to the fact that the Lord said that Father Whelan is a beacon and a light to heal the nation.

The lives of the saints are full of stories how God selects certain holy and humble people to give them special gifts. Father, now Monsignor William Whelan is one of those people. St. Therese of Liseaux was one of those people. She lived a young life in a cloistered convent in France with no contact with the public, but her passion and love for the Lord so enamored him with her that he allowed thousands of miracles to happen through her intercession after her death.

Father Whelan describes himself in the title of his book as: *An Ordinary Priest Gifted by God's Grace.* His book can be ordered from Standard Press in Omaha. Father Whelan, like the late Father Thomas Halley, S.J., was an ordinary priest whom God loved, who has great love for God and his people. I have been so blessed to have these saintly men in my life.

CHAPTER 18: VIRGIN VICTORIOUS APPEARING IN MISSOURI

Last year after Mass and the rosary I visited with my new friend Grace Ann Ancona. A group of us went to the chapel after Mass each day and prayed the rosary together, both women and men. I learned that Grace Ann had been to Medjugorje because during her recitation of one decade of the rosary with us, she prayed to "Our Lady of Medjugorje." This brought up the conversation afterward that she had just been to Medjugorje. It turned out that in addition to Grace Ann, five of us in that chapel that day had also been to Medjugorje including one husband and wife. We were all called, and somehow Our Lady made sure we had the money to go.

After the others left, Grace Ann told me about a holy place in Climax Spring, Missouri where a very holy woman named Lory Bremner holds prayer services every Thursday. Mrs. Bremner started having visions of the Blessed Mother in Medjugorje when she went on a pilgrimage there, I believe in 1996. When she returned, both the Blessed Mother and Our Lord appeared to her and gave her messages to share and they continued to appear to her with messages until sometime in 2011. She also had visions from many of the saints. She had total recall of the conversations she had with the Blessed Mother, Our Lord and the saints and wrote down their messages. Her bishop did not discourage her prayer days and her spiritual director advised her to publish the messages. Booklets with these messages can be purchased for the mailing cost alone. There are two separate booklets each for Our Lord and Our Lady and booklets on the messages from the saints.

I traveled with Grace Ann and Helen Boos and Shirley Fischer to Climax Springs to attend a Thursday day of prayer. Thursday is the day for public prayer. Lory's apparitions when she returned continued in Lees Summit where she used to live until Our Lady told her and her husband Dick to find a place in southern Missouri. They purchased an acreage. They have built a chapel with a meeting room attached to the chapel.

On that Thursday we prayed the Stations of the Cross in the chapel. After a small lunch, we prayed the rosary out loud together outside facing the grotto and the statue of the Virgin Victorious, the name the Blessed Mother told Lory to call her, and later in the chapel we prayed together again. After the rosary, Lory read one of the messages she was given earlier. This one was from Our Lord. She discussed the meaning of the message and asked for discussion. In the morning we had been given pieces of paper to write the names of the people we were praying for and we placed these papers in a silver basket. Lory spoke out loud to the Blessed Mother when we went out to the grotto to pray the rosary and asked her to intercede with Jesus for the people we were praying for and for us. She placed the silver basket near the statue of the Virgin Victorious before starting to pray the rosary.

We had a break for coffee, fruit and rolls, where we got to visit with Lory after she read some of the messages that Our Lord and Our Lady gave her previously. I got to sit near her and ask her when she first started to have her apparitions. That's when she told me that they started when she went to Medjugorje. I told her that I was writing a book about the pilgrimage my mother and I took there in 1988 and would she give me permission to write about her story. She gave me permission.

We could take as many copies of the booklets containing the messages. I took some to send to Helen in Omaha. I called her and told her about my visit to Lory and Yahweh Shalom, the name Lory gave to their land and the Chapel. I read all of my copies when I got home. The messages are so beautiful.

I went a few times more with Helen and Shirley. One of the things we did before we left each Thursday to go back home was to go up to the five feet crucifix on the property. It had been blessed by Our Lord and Our Lady. And people received healings from these prayers. Those of us who wanted to be prayed over would gather around the crucifix and one by one Lory would put one hand on Our Lord's arm on the crucifix and one hand on each of us and prayed over us. One time after she prayed over me she said: "You must be very special." I asked her why and she said: "because Our Lady appeared behind you while I prayed over you." I felt very blessed and humbled. Lory still has visions and inner locutions or inner speakings but not apparitions. The apparitions stopped in 2011.

I called Lory one night last month to confirm her address and website and phone number. You can write to her with your prayer intentions and you can order copies of the booklets with the messages. You only have to pay the postage. The booklets are not for sale. She gets donations to print the messages. You can also access her website at www.yahwehshalom-VirginVictorious.com to read the messages and to order the booklets. And

184

Sundance and Cherokee Moon

you can call her with your prayer requests for the Blessed Mother at 1-573-345-4710. Lory may have to have volunteers help her take the phone calls when many people call her like they called Father Peter Mary Rookey in Chicago.

I was able to go back to Yahweh Sholom August 21, 2014, with Shirley and Helen and a woman named Mary Ann. Helen, Mary Ann and I were able to attend 7:00 Mass said by a healing priest from Africa at a nursing home where he says Mass every day at 7:00 a.m. He also says an 11:00 Mass at a hospital. We then drove to meet Shirley and rode with her to Yahweh Shalom. Wednesday, the night before, I hand wrote on both sides of an 8 ½ by 11 sheet of paper in columns all the names of the people I wanted Our Lord and Our Lady to bless. In the chapel we say the Stations of the Cross and other prayers and outdoors we say the rosary in front of the statue of Virgin Victorious.

Afterward the able bodied among us knelt next to the statute and kissed the two stones where Our Lord and Our Lady appeared for years to Lory. The only expense of visiting Yahweh Shalom is your gas plus any meals you have on the way or back. It is a three hour drive for us from the intersection of Highway 291 and I-70 East toward St. Louis to Highway 7 south to Yahweh Shalom. Remember, Thursday is the day for public prayer. You should be there by 10:10 a.m. for prayer at the five foot healing cross.

CHAPTER 19: THE NATIONAL SCANDAL REGARDING MENTAL ILLNESS, AND NAMI, AN ADVOCACY ORGANIZATION

My lawsuit against the County Attorney and the Public Defender was one of many lawsuits filed in the United States challenging State mental health commitment laws and to stop the automatic warehousing of people with mental illness in State mental hospitals. Part of the national movement for change was to close these state hospitals where mistreatment of the patients and other horrors were happening.

I even appeared before the health and welfare committee of the Nebraska legislature as one of several witnesses about closing the State mental hospitals at Norfolk and Hastings. These two cities were in outstate Nebraska. Most of the patients came from the big cities of Omaha and Lincoln. I argued that the state should build smaller short term hospitals in Omaha and Lincoln with extensive community based treatment and it should end the warehousing of people in these remote cities. I urged the legislature to provide economic relief to help find other businesses for these two communities who relied on these large state institutions as the major employer in their cities.

I noted that because of new psychiatric medications patients could be released back into their communities with community based support. One of the witnesses who agreed that new medications were helping was a woman psychiatrist. But she warned that it was too soon to close the hospitals and agreed that community based treatment was crucial.

A few years later, the hospitals were closed as mental hospitals, not because the State was going to provide smaller hospitals in urban areas and community based treatment, but to cut the budget. Not only did the state not provide these smaller State hospitals, but two private hospitals St. Joseph Mental Hospital and Richard Young Mental Hospital in Omaha, both where I had been hospitalized before, had to close because the State would not give them adequate reimbursement for patient care. Years later, a new organization took over the Richard Young facility. The hospital is called the Island of Hope.

Closing large State mental hospitals and failing to provide funds for private hospitals and community based treatment became a national trend and a national scandal. Worse than that, it has become impossible to obtain mental health commitment for people who do need this temporary care. The legal standard is that the individual must be suicidal or homicidal. But the standard that is enforced is that they have to be in the process of these acts in front of a psychiatrist or government official such as the police. The standard is so strict that people are being denied treatment.

As reported this year on the CBS program *60 Minutes* which was rerun June 7th, 2014, we have turned our prisons into the new mental hospitals and they are not equipped to provide mental health treatment nor funded for this treatment. The head of the Chicago County jail reported on the show that 80% of his inmates are mentally ill. He asked if prison is really better than a mental hospital for mentally ill people.

Nebraska amended their law to provide for outpatient mental health commitment where the person has to take daily medications to comply with the commitment. Nebraska does not have a mental health court for mentally ill persons who are arrested. Nebraska does have alcohol and drug addiction courts where treatment is required to avoid conviction and I understand that they now have a diversion program in Douglas County, the county where Omaha is located..

Missouri, where I presently live, has a mental health court only in Jackson County including Kansas City, but does not provide outpatient mental health commitment. Like in Nebraska and most States, in Missouri it is nearly impossible to get someone committed. In Missouri, it is the doctor who has to file. A family member cannot file for commitment like they do in Nebraska.

Missouri law also provides for a 96 hour police hold when a person is in a mental illness episode that brings the person to the police attention so they can be evaluated but the person has to agree to be held. It really means nothing. There needs to be increased funding here and outpatient commitment and statewide mental health courts. Like in Nebraska and elsewhere, the city and county jails do not provide treatment except in Jackson County. Missouri. There are three State prisons in Missouri that do provide treatment.

There has to be some half way procedure to get mentally ill people help between warehousing and jails. I heard former Congressman Patrick Kennedy addressing this situation on National Public Television by proposing a new legal standard, i.e., the right to be well. Congress was considering such a bill, but there were serious privacy rights issues with the legislation. A change in the standard will provide nothing if the federal and state governments fail to provide adequate funding for mental health care.

It is going to take the election and reelection of concerned and responsible lawmakers for the funding and legal standard changes to be made and that will only happen by citizen pressure on lawmakers and the defeat of lawmakers who ignore this national crisis and obstruct proposed legislation and public pressure on federal and state governments.

Beside becoming informed, advocating for funding and legislative changes and defeating obstructionist lawmakers, individuals can pay the $35.00 regular annual membership cost by joining N.A.M.I. (the National Alliance on Mental Illness). Besides being the main lobby organization for mentally ill people like me and for our families, N.A.M.I. provides literature and programs for us and our families and programs to help eradicate stigma and another program to train police officers in the treatment of persons with mental illness who come into contact with law enforcement. If you Google or search "NAMI membership information," you will obtain information for all kinds of help including legal representation.

N.A.M.I. of Kansas City got a grant to train local police officers in how to handle mentally ill people who come into contact with law enforcement. It has been very successful. The police here in Lees Summit are trained and do a good job too. But like most police officers, they are frustrated by the mental health system and lack of services.

To become a member of NAMI, Google or search: "NAMI membership" or call NAMI 1-800-950-NAMI (6264).

CHAPTER 20: 380 MILLION WORLDWIDE AND 60 MILLION PEOPLE A YEAR IN AMERICA SUFFER MENTAL ILLNESS AND 38,000 SUICIDES OCURRED IN 2013 IN AMERICA ALONE

These are the statistics that internationally renowned Pastor Rick Warren (author of *The Purpose Driven Life*) and his wife Kay cited in their opinion piece in *Time Magazine* March 27, 2014. They obtained these statistics from NAMI who obtained them from the National Institute for Mental Illness, a U.S. government agency under the Department of Health and the World Health Organization. The facts are that 60 million people a year suffer from some form of mental illness in America, and in 2013, 38,000 people committed suicide. The statistics for the world from the World Health Organization are that 380 million people suffer from mental illness worldwide each year.

The Warrens are painfully aware of these statistics because their beloved son Matthew committed suicide in an impulse after attending a family gathering earlier in the day. Matthew had suffered mental illness from the time he was seven years old. He had professional care from age seven and had ups and downs during his life. His family was shocked and saddened by his death.

The Warrens were open about this tragedy for their son and the outpouring of condolences was overwhelming. Eleven months later they sponsored a national conference with the website www.mentalhealthandthechurch.com. The conference initiated a national call to the churches to further inspire the churches to help people with mental illness and their families since many families turn to their priests and pastors first in these crises. Often the church officials are the first responders.

The Warrens also lifted the veil over mental illness by showing that it is in fact an illness not a character flaw. People can't just "snap out of it." Knowledge of what little mental health resources exist is crucial for the faith community as well as the community at large and advocating for greater funding and more programs and doctors is crucial.

Suicide can be planned out of desperation and it can be an immediate impulse. One should never dismiss someone's talk about suicide. This talk is a cry for help. In an issue of *Psychology Today* magazine, reported on line without citation, Dr. Lisa Firestone, Ph.D. wrote an article titled "Suicide: The Warning Signs." She lists nine warning signs:

1. Disrupted sleep. Sometimes people who commit suicide have not slept for weeks.
2. Isolation. The person pushes away family and friends.
3. Loss of Interest: The person gives up activities that previously gave him or her pleasure.
4. Extreme self-hatred: A downward spiral of self-destructive behavior.
5. Extreme self-denial: Lacking any pleasure.
6. Not belonging: A feeling that no one cares.
7. Being a burden to others: being told what a burden one is to family or friends.
8. A sudden positive mood change: This is a sign that one has made the decision to commit suicide to end the pain and suffering.
9. Suicidal talk: Always take this seriously. It is a call for help.
10. The National Suicide Prevention Lifeline is 1-800-273-TALK (8255). Share it with others.

My first encounter with suicide was when I was in seventh grade at St .Peter's Grade School in Omaha, Nebraska. We had a set of twin boys in our class. Everyone liked them. One day one of the brothers had what I later learned was an epileptic seizure in the hallway in front of the whole class. A few days later he hung himself in the basement of his home with a close line. We were all devastated.

The next time I encountered suicide was when I worked in the Douglas County Juvenile Court where I worked for Judge Joseph Moylan. Judge Moylan's court reporter committed suicide. We were all shocked. He gave no sign of depression. We grieved for him.

The third time I almost witnessed a suicide in the Douglas County Court House. From the second floor up to the sixth floor there is an open circular space surrounded on each floor with a round marble railing, the space is called the rotunda. One day I was on the third floor talking to Ed Fogarty. I was facing him looking east at the office of the Clerk of the District Court. Ed was facing me looking west toward the Probate Court office. All of a sudden I saw a woman rushing out of the Clerk's office.

Sundance and Cherokee Moon

She ran up to the railing and was leaning over it as if she was contemplating jumping. I immediately directed Ed to her with my eyes and the expression of horror on my face. He immediately backed up and over to where she was and grabbed her just as she was trying to jump. Ed saved her life.

Ironically that evening my friends, my girls and I were eating at the Olive Garden Restaurant near 73rd and Dodge Street in Omaha. At the next table people were talking about this rescue. From the conversation, they were relatives of the husband. One of them cursed the man who saved her and wished that she had died. Apparently the husband and wife were in the process of divorce. I was shocked by that callous statement. I called Ed the next day and reported the shocking conversation with him. I always wondered what happened to that woman. Did she get help? Did she live?

Then as I reported earlier, my friend Dave Liddell committed suicide. I had another friend, a woman friend who shared my bi-polar illness like Dave, who failed in her first suicide attempt and years later was successful after she was dying of cancer.

191

CHAPTER 21: ROBIN WILLIAMS AND FATHER DAMIEN

Recently, the much beloved and famous actor/comedian Robin Williams committed suicide. It appears from the facts of his death that he committed suicide in an impulse from despair. He had been diagnosed with Parkinson's disease. And afterward a doctor explained in the media that profound depression can accompany Parkinson's disease. It was later verified that he had another disease that affected his brain and thinking. Robin Williams was a much loved comedian and serious and comedic actor with television and film contributions.

One of Robin Williams lesser known artistic efforts is as narrator of the documentary on the life of Saint Father Damien of Molokai. Robin's effort was an effort of love. Father Damien was a priest from Belgium who went to Hawaii and the island of Molockai to pastor to the people with leprosy who were forced to live on the island in the Kalaupapa Leprosy Settlement. Because of the infectious nature of this horrible disease without any cure at the time, victims of it were quarantined on the island and neglected.

Father Damien ministered to these people, treated them with every respect and love and was much loved by his people. Word of his holiness and the efforts he was making for these forgotten and neglected people spread worldwide, and money for services for the people was sent to the settlement. Years later, Father Damien succumbed to the disease himself. Many, many years later there was a cure for the disease which became known as Hansen's disease.

The film is titled *The Father Damien Story: An Uncommon Kindness* and the film depicts Father Damien's life from his days in Belgium through his missionary work in Molokai to his death, his beatification and canonization in the Roman Catholic Church. Father Damien was and is revered by ordinary people and by Presidents and Kings including Ghandi and President Roosevelt. A statue of Father Damien stands in the United States Congressional Statutory Hall in Washington, D.C. (The DVD is available on Amazon.)

I have this wonderful picture in my head of Father Damien greeting Robin Williams upon his death with his arms around him.

CHAPTER 22: OUR LADY OF THE PRESENTATION PARISH, A BLUE RIBBON PARISH

One of the outcomes of this horrendous priest pedophile scandal is that it over shadows the thousands of good and holy priests. I can testify that all the priests in my life from kindergarten to this day were and are good and holy priests. These priests from Blessed Sacrament, St. Peter's, and St. Margaret Mary's, Immaculate Conception and Sacred Heart parishes I belonged to in Omaha, the Jesuits at Creighton University, Father Bill Whelan, Father Thomas Halley, S.J., to Holy Spirit and Abbot Barnabas Senecal in Overland Park, Kansas, and the priests at St. Francis Xavier, the Jesuit parish, in Kansas City, MO, and most recently, the priests of Our Lady of the Presentation here in Lees Summit, MO, Father Michael Cleary and now Father Tom Holder and our associates—all have been and are good and holy priests.

I have been a parishioner at Our Lady of the Presentation since 2009 since I have lived in Lees Summit, MO. Our Lady of the Presentation is the largest parish in the Kansas City-St. Joseph, MO diocese. It is a vibrant parish and the Saturday evening and Sunday Masses are packed. The parish and the parents support what the federal government has awarded as a National Blue Ribbon School. The recent award was given to the school based on student achievement and faculty. Our Lady of the Presentation School is one of fifty private schools nationwide to receive this honor.

Our school was also the winner of the K-Mart Education Award of $500,000.00 in its national education prize contest. The parishioners and everyone we knew including soldiers in Afghanistan voted to make this school number one. The priests before them and Father Michael Cleary, our former pastor, and Father Tom Holder, our current pastor can take great credit for the vibrancy of this parish and its parishioners. They are small "c" charismatic, dedicated, and holy priests. The Catholic Church will survive because of priests like these and a dedicated following of Catholics of all political persuasions.

I am at an age when I have the time to be involved in many aspects of Parish life including being a member of the St. Joseph Guild which provides funeral lunches and supports women and children in shelters and contributes food to the local social service agencies. And most often, I can participate daily at Mass and joining a group of women and men to say the rosary after Mass weekdays. I have made many friends in this parish.

Our current pope, Pope Francis, through his holiness and love for all people has revitalized the Catholic Church worldwide. Reactionaries call him a communist for his economic policies. They are the policies of Jesus. Pope Francis embodies the life of Jesus Christ who loves all people and preached conversion, forgiveness and mercy, and Pope Francis has made the Church more inclusive. The media has named him the Pope of the world. May he have a long and fruitful life, and may the Church hierarchy follow his example.

CHAPTER 23: I AM A MERMAID

On a lighter note, I must confess that I am a mermaid. I am a member of a water aerobics class in Kansas City. We call ourselves the Mermaids. My sister Therese and her husband Paul got me to join the Mermaids when I was having trouble with my lower back so much that I had to get help to get out of bed I was in so much pain. I was taking a series of shots in my lower spine but the real help came when I would come seven days a week for water therapy. The women and the few men, many in their 90's, in the class bonded and we all became friends. We got physical therapy in the water and good conversation and emotional support. Some of us get together out of class. And we have a summer party and a January party. Some of us go to lunch together regularly and to the movies.

One of our beloved Mermaid friends Joanna Douglas had a long struggle with cancer. She had several surgeries. She continued to come to the pool whenever she could. Joanna was a hugger. Whenever she came into the pool area, we always clapped and cheered for her. She would get into the water and go around and give all of us hugs.

Before Joanna died from cancer a few years ago after a long struggle, she told her daughters she wanted the Mermaids to speak at her funeral. When we all entered the church, we saw that her daughters had made posters with all of our pictures on them and the bold words: "The Mermaids." We were all asked to come up front on the altar after her pastor spoke her eulogy. We chose Melba Meyers to be our spokesperson. That year in 2012, I also lost my friends Carole Barnes and her sister JoAnn Williams to cancer.

CHAPTER 24: TELL ME YOUR STORY

It is my goal to publish the stories of other people: stories of other people who have survived mental illness; stories of people who have been to Medjugorje or other holy places and the impact of these visits on their lives; stories of people whose spirituality helped them in their search for mental, emotional and physical wellness; stories of miracles and/ or spiritual and/ or mystical experiences people have had.

Try to put your story into five typed pages or 1250 words if possible. Give me written permission to use your story. You keep all rights to your own stories; you are just going to let me use them.

Give me your name, address, phone number and email address and tell me if you want me to publish any or all of this information if you want people to be able to contact you.

I can be contacted at Mary Kay Green, Sr., c/o Mary Kay Green, Jr., 402 NE Corder Street, Lees Summit, MO 64063 or by email at mkgkansascity17@gmail.com. If you email me, leave your phone number and I will try to call you if you are in the United States.

If you like my book, make a comment on Amazon below my book information. Search for me at Google or Bing or your other search engines: "Mary Kay Green" or "Mary Kay Green, J.D." I am not Mary Kay Green, the judge from Texas or the cosmetics Mary Kay salesperson named Mary Kay Green. My webpage is www.marykaygreen.com.

Go to YOU TUBE to watch my soon to be uploaded videos about my story and this book at: "Sundance and Cherokee Moon." Watch my interview with Crystal Chambers Stewart on YOU TUBE at "Women of Courage the Rights of Single Mothers." You can also search for Crystal Chambers v. The Omaha Girls Club on your computers. Check Amazon by my name Mary Kay Green, J.D. for my other books to be published in 2015 including my screenplay *They Let Mothers in Law School and my book At Will/No Deal: The Civil Rights Laws Exceptions to At Will Employment.*

CHAPTER 25: I AM AVAILABLE TO SPEAK

I am available to speak about my life with mental illness, to educate people about the issues facing mentally ill people like myself, particularly for the young people, to advocate for changes in the law and for increased funding for mental health treatment and to help end the stigma associated with mental illness. I am now one of the public faces of mental illness.

I am available to speak about my spiritual life and experiences and how my spirituality, good and holy priests and nuns, along with good doctors, especially my psychiatrist Dr. A. Mohammed Mirza, M.D., good medications and the love and support of my daughters Mary Kay and Elizabeth and my grandchildren Ms. Phelan and Michael and my family and my friends helped me to triumph over mental illness. I am available to offer hope and love and encouragement to others.

I am available to talk about the Blessed Mother and Medjugorje and her messages. And I am available to talk about the role of spirituality and prayer in our lives.

I am available to encourage young people to get help and to know that there are dedicated psychiatrists, doctors and therapists who can help and neuroscientists who are working on non-drug treatments of both mental and physical illnesses. Some of the current drugs have serious side effects and some do not.

At the end of the movie *The Song of Bernadette,* Bernadette's parish priest looks out at the audience and says: "To those who believe, no explanation is necessary. To those who don't believe, no explanation is sufficient." That's a Bible quote as well.

CONTACT ME at mkgkansascity17@gmail.com. I will check my emails every day. Otherwise, write to me: Mary Kay Green, J.D. Author, c/o Mary Kay Green, Jr., 402 NE Corder Street, Lees Summit, MO 64063.

Thank you, dear readers. As that late great film critic Roger Ebert always said: "See you at the movies."

There is an old Irish blessing: "May you be in heaven six hours before the devil knows you are there." Mary Kay Green, J.D.

PHOTOS

Robert Redford taken at Omaha, Nebraska fundraiser

Me at Sundance Film Festival with Louise Levison and a friend

Cliff Robertson at Sundance

The Key to the City Of Omaha to the Blessed Virgin Mary

Father Thomas Halley, S.J. and me presenting the Key to the City of Omaha to Our Lady at the crucifix on Apparition Hill.

Father Halley saying Mass at Mount Krezevic or Cross Mountain

My mother in the grey and white stripped top and Father Halley

Rosemary, her mother, her sister and her aunt with Father Halley

Our hosts Rosa and George's family

St. James Church in Medjugorje

My photo of the statue of the Blessed Mother at Caritas near where the Blessed Mother appeared to Marija and I witnessed her talking to the Blessed Mother

Sundance and Cherokee Moon

Made in the USA
Coppell, TX
12 April 2021